SPANISH-AMERICAN INSTITUTE: THE FIRST FORTY-ONE YEARS— A RETROSPECTIVE

Together we made a difference:
The true story of the birth, growth,
and development of an educational institution

Frank J. Ferraro

VANTAGE PRESS
New York

Quotes from *New York Paramount Theatre*, Annual No. 3, © 1976, reprinted with permission by the publisher: Theatre Historical Society of America, Inc., Elmhurst, Illinois.

FIRST EDITION

All rights reserved, including the right of reproduction in whole or in part in any form.

Copyright © 2004 by Frank J. Ferraro

Published by Vantage Press, Inc.
419 Park Ave. South, New York, NY 10016

Manufactured in the United States of America
ISBN: 0-533-14808-1

Library of Congress Catalog Card No.: 2003098788

0 9 8 7 6 5 4 3 2 1

To the many who helped along the way and especially Matthew Connelly, who served tirelessly as project research assistant.

*The Master in the art of living makes little
distinction between his work and his play,
his labor and his leisure, his mind and his body,
his education and his recreation, his love and
his religion. He hardly knows which is which.
He simply pursues his vision of excellence in
whatever he does, leaving others to decide
whether he is working or playing. To him he
is always doing both.*

—Zen Buddhist text

Preface

The subject of this narrative concerns the birth, evolution, and development of an educational institution . . . but in addition, some information about the co-founders: Frank J. Ferraro and David Schiffman should be made known to the reader from the outset.

Both were born in 1926 . . . Dave on January 1 and Frank on March 1 . . . and both were raised in the Borough of Brooklyn: Dave in Borough Park and Frank in Bensonhurst. They both attended public schools in their respective areas and upon graduation became classmates at the New Utrecht High School, although they circulated among different schoolmates and except that they were slightly aware of each other, had little personal contact during their high school years.

Upon graduation in June of 1944, they were both inducted into the U.S. Army, though assigned to different units. Both were granted honorable discharges in 1946, and both took immediate steps to attend college under the G.I. Bill: Dave at Hunter College and Frank at Adelphi College after his transfer from Bergen Junior College (years later, Fairleigh Dickinson University). Dave's major was in English literature, and Frank majored in English with a minor in Journalism. Dave graduated Hunter with a B.A. degree and Phi Beta Kappa honors. Frank graduated Adelphi with a B.A. degree.

At this point Dave was single . . . Frank already married with a wonderful wife and two beautiful children. Both sought employment in an economic period that was not very fertile for young aspiring teachers . . . so they did the best they could . . . and both were advised by different counselors that "one MUST" in these times go for a master's degree.

There were far too many B.A.s around . . . and so Dave enrolled in the master's degree program at the New York University Graduate School of Arts and Science. Frank, on the receiving end of the same advice from his sources registered in the master's degree program at the Graduate School of Arts and Science, New York University. Both attended in the evening session, and both, sharing the same major, recalled old times and actually developed a relationship as friends, which continued for the next forty plus years.

Eventually Frank landed employment as a provisional New York City Welfare Department investigator. It was a "step up" in a very tight job market. Frank told Dave, after which he too became a provisional investigator with the New York City Department of Welfare.

Sometime later, Frank was appointed to the faculty of Fairleigh Dickinson University . . . as a part-time English instructor . . . thanks to the recommendation of Professor MacEachen, a really great friend and human being, who had admired his efforts as a student. The appointment lasted about two-and-one-half years . . . and was not renewed by FDU because there would have had to be a full-time appointment with credit towards tenure if the employment continued, and the university was not disposed to such an offer at that time. But during Frank's employment, he recommended Dave to a part-time position at FDU. Dave did receive the appointment, but didn't renew after a semester or two.

Finally, both Dave and Frank responded to an ad for an English teacher that appeared in the *New York Times.* It was for evening session in a private school, the Fernandez Bi-Lingual Institute, located on 42nd Street near 6th Avenue.

Both Dave and Frank submitted résumés (separately), including transcripts. Both men waited . . . but only Dave was called for an interview. He appeared . . . was interviewed ... but when he was informed that the salary would be $1.00 per hour for three hours work, five evenings weekly from 6:00 to 9:00 P.M., he gratefully rejected the opportunity.

Dave related his experience to Frank ... they were somewhat taken aback. ... Frank the more so because he had paid $2.00 for the copy of his transcript and felt that if there was no chance for the job, he might as well visit the school and request the return of the transcript. Having received the name and address of the school from Dave (we had previously responded to a post office box number), Frank did stop in to meet and request the return of his transcript from Mr. Fernandez, the director. Mr. Fernandez, who barely spoke English, rummaged around in his file cabinet until he admitted that he could not find Frank's material or transcript ... and in the process asked Frank if he was interested in the position. He said that he was and, miracle of miracles, was hired on the spot, right then and there, no further questions asked.

Frank remained in that position for three years ... expanding hours and duties ... increasing salary ... but most of all expanding experience at the same time that the seeds were planted, leading eventually to the desire to establish a school of one's own. In the years that followed, Frank had expressed to many friends and colleagues the prospect of starting a school: they were all college grads ... each could be effective in his/her area of education ... they all liked the idea ... but when March 1, 1955 drew closer, it was Dave who in very clear simple terms: "Frank, if you ever start a school, I'd like to play a part in it." That's about all he said ... and that's about how it was.

Frank Ferraro

Introduction

On March 1, 1955, the Spanish-American Institute opened its doors to the public. It was established as a private school teaching English as a second language to the large influx of men and women entering the U.S. from Latin America, the islands, especially Puerto Rico, the Dominican Republic, and Cuba. At the same time the Institute offered courses in secretarial subjects so that a foreign-born student might prepare for employment at the same time that he or she was gaining English-language proficiency.

But I am getting a bit ahead of the story: some statistics will put the birth of this institution into proper perspective. The administration consisted of Frank J. Ferraro and David Schiffman. The faculty consisted of two: Ferraro, a graduate of Adelphi University (B.A.) and a Master of Arts Degree from New York University Graduate School of Arts and Science. Schiffman, a graduate of Hunter College (B.A.) and a Master of Arts Degree from New York University Graduate School of Arts and Science.

From the first that I started to formulate the idea of starting a school, David was interested. I had discussed the plan with more than a few other young, intelligent friends, but in the end it was David alone who clearly let me know that he was interested in participating if I really planned to go ahead with the plan. And so it was that although I was the instigator, Dave remained my best right hand throughout the next forty years.

Planning was the first order of business. Much of that took place in my own mind. Various ideas . . . some practical, some very idealistic . . . how to create the perfect language center. How to attract students . . . how to improve upon methods I had been exposed to in a language school for which I was employed as an instructor of English as a second language . . . what about textbooks . . . what about money. Money? How much and where on earth was it to come from? And then location . . . Location . . . LOCATION! Where the heck could the school be located? Money and location: a sensible plan to begin.

NOW ABOUT THE MONEY: The first best place to start in quest of start-up money was THE SELF . . . Frank and Dave . . . after all, it was to be our baby!

Frank and Dave . . . the money . . . THE MONEY?

I had the grand total of $500, that's five hundred dollars to my good name . . . a good wife and two great children to support. Five hundred dollars as my start-up capital . . . to establish a school while at the same time caring for my wife and children. Five hundred dollars! Where does one begin? A conference: Dear wife . . . I know what . . . I'll take two hundred fifty dollars for start-up money. You hang on to the remaining two hundred fifty . . . use it . . . stretch it as far as you can . . . stretch it as only you can and when you need some, let me know and I should have some for you and my two children. That was the plan. Approved by my supporting wife . . . unbeknownst to my two children. And that's how Frank raised his part of the start-up money.

Now about Dave . . . the money and HIS PART.

I must digress a moment to inform you that amongst some segments of American society it is accepted as a fact that all humans of Jewish extraction are extremely wealthy and it follows that the children of these humans are born with golden or at least silver spoons in their mouths. Now it must be noted that Dave in 1955 was a young Jewish man of Jewish parentage. Need I write more? Our quest for start-up money . . . let's look to Dave . . . the gold or silver spoon? Now about Dave . . . the money and HIS PART:

Quite simply put: HE HAD NONE!

Dave was NOT the son of wealthy parents. His father had passed away years ago ... but he had the most wonderful mother money couldn't buy. There was an insurance policy ... with a face value of $250. There's that magic number again ... TWO HUNDRED FIFTY DOLLARS from Dave's insurance policy and TWO HUNDRED FIFTY DOLLARS from Frank's family nest egg went together to total FIVE HUNDRED DOLLARS ... ENOUGH TO START A SCHOOL on March 1, 1955 ... in the greatest city in the world ... located in the United States of America ... the greatest country in the world!

We had the MONEY. But now ... LOCATION ... LOCATION ... LOCATION.

WHERE?

Without question the best location was in Times Square ... the Crossroads of the World! Best because of the marvelous mass transit system: subway ... bus ... which made every part of the city: Brooklyn, Queens, Bronx, Staten Island, and even parts of the state of New Jersey, easily accessible to our anticipated student population.

Times Square ... The Crossroads of the World, which would be most likely familiar in the minds of the newly arrived to our shores ... those who spoke little (or no) English and probably less able to get around many parts of the city ... but Times Square ... the Crossroads of the world ... NO PROBLEM ... almost any person had been so much exposed, through motion pictures and familiar photos to feel at home in Times Square.

So that was it: location ... Location ... LOCATION! And now to find the spot. How to do that? On our budget ... no real estate agents ... no newspaper, radio, or TV ads ... it was a simple case of personal footwork ... a survey of buildings from street to street ... avenue to avenue ... head bent sideways with eyes scanning windows . . . space for rent . . . office space available, for lease . . . inquire within: the super. Up and down each street from Fortieth to Forty fifth Street . . . Sixth Avenue to Eighth Avenue . . . where to find a space not too close to the many many porno shops that dominated the area in the 1950s.

Fortieth Street . . . Forty first Street . . . Forty third Street . . . oops, wait . . . Forty second Street: there was the sign in the windows . . . space available on the twelfth floor of a narrow red brick building . . . twelve stories high, not more than 35 to 40 feet wide . . . space available, inquire within, Super. On 42nd Street about 150 feet from the corner . . . the south-east side of the street, right next to the blaring marquee of an adult porno theater!

What the hell . . . in our situation ONE CAN'T HAVE EVERYTHING . . . so I went in to see the space at 140 West 42nd Street, just off Seventh Avenue in Times Square . . . the crossroads of the world!

The entrance was narrow . . . the lobby narrow and dingy at the end of which were two small self-service elevators and beyond a narrow stairway with iron steps and railings for those who would prefer to climb.

The super was on the second floor. I walked up and after informing him of my interest in the vacant space, he went with me by elevator to the twelfth floor. The space consisted of three rooms, each set off of a narrow hallway on the south side of the building. The rooms seemed suitable for our purposes.

"How much is the rent?" I asked.

"I don't know," the reply. "You have to talk to the owner, Mr. Silverman. He's at his main office on 38th Street and 7th Avenue" . . . afterwhich he gave me the exact address and I went directly to speak with Mr. Silverman. AND WHAT AN EXPERIENCE!

The building, between 37th and 38th Street on 7th Avenue . . . the heart of the garment industry . . . a wide building eight to ten floors . . . a very large lobby with two elevators. I entered and pressed for the fourth floor and Mr. Silverman.

The elevator doors opened to a very large and very wide open loft area with many garment racks scattered about in what appeared to be no apparent order . . . and about ten to fifteen steps beyond the elevators a very large desk . . . and behind the desk the receptionist, whom I later came to know as Mrs. K.

"May I help you?"

I nodded "yes" and took those steps closer to the desk. "I'm interested in the space on 42nd Street. The three rooms on the twelfth floor."

She turned quickly toward a person at the far end of the large loft area. . . . "It's about the 42nd Street space," she called loudly to him. The person, with a quick wave of his hand, and without looking in our direction: "Send him over," he said. And that was Mr. Silverman.

Mr. Silverman was a tall man . . . one or two inches above six feet . . . broad chested . . . well combed head of hair . . . a well-pressed pair of slacks . . . white shirt, opened at the collar . . . no tie . . . long sleeves turned up at the cuffs so that they were wrist length. From his neck, three tape measures and a cloth hung freely and as I drew closer I could see the cloth contained a large quantity of pins.

In the next moment, as I approached Mr. Silverman, three or four models appeared from behind several clothing racks and made their way quickly to where he stood. Mr. Silverman tucked a sleeve on one of the dresses . . . pinned a collar on another and quickly drew a belt more snugly around the waist of a third. His movements were rapid . . . automatic.

"The space on 42nd Street," he said without looking directly at me. "You've seen it?"

"Yes, the super. I think it's good for our purpose."

"What business?" he asked.

"A school."

"A school?" He seemed to glance my way quickly. "What kind of school?"

"English language," I said. "And probably some business subjects . . . typing, bookkeeping . . . things like that. How much is the rent?"

"Two hundred six a month."

"We can do that," I responded happily. "We want to begin on March 1st."

Mr. Silverman turned facing the desk and Mrs. K near the elevator and without breaking his stride . . . "K give him a receipt for four hundred twelve dollars and the keys to 42nd Street, twelfth floor."

My heart sank. "I thought the rent was two hundred six." I said.

"It is. One month's security and one month's rent."

My hopes were dashed. "I can't do that."

"Well, what did you have in mind?" Silverman.

"I thought I'd give two-hundred six dollars for March rent. Get the school going. Then April 1st pay $206 rent and $206 each month as we go along."

I don't know exactly what Mr. Silverman thought as he glanced quickly down at me. And then . . . "K give him a receipt for $206 and the keys."

I think I floated across the space to the desk . . . placed the rent in cash . . . all 206 dollars of it on the desk before Mrs. K . . . plunged the receipt and the keys into my pocket . . . pressed the elevator door "down" button . . . in an instant, the doors slid open . . . I stepped gingerly in and as the doors began to close behind me . . . a voice from the far end of the room: Mr. Silverman.

"Good luck, kid. See you in April."

The doors shut. The elevator descended. The doors opened . . . the lobby . . . floating out the building's front exit . . .

"Wow . . . we've got a place . . . we'll have a school. Who would believe?"

1

On March 1, 1955, the school was opened and except for the fact that we had no students, everything was great. We had in the weeks prior to the opening struggled to hit upon a suitable name . . . and we went through a considerable number: The American English Language Institute . . . The School of English and Commerce . . . The Institute of Secretarial and English Language Studies . . . and on and on and on. Nothing seemed to ring just right. There was the Berlitz School . . . a Latin-American Institute . . . a Bi-Lingual Institute . . . and Lord knows what else. We tried and tried . . . and thought and thought and then WHAM . . . SPANISH-AMERICAN INSTITUTE!!

The Spanish-American Institute. It sounded so right. It rang so true. Why had it taken so long? Would it be open to use or had someone already laid claim to it? It was so natural, could it really be available? We contacted a young lawyer friend, Leo Darzy, who filed the necessary forms with the State of New York, and in what seemed like no time flat, we were notified that the name was clear and now properly registered for use by Frank J. Ferraro and David Schiffman as a private school operating in the State of New York.

A bit more about Leo Darzy. A really good friend. A young and very promising lawyer who did so very much for our plans as they developed. He gave us legal advice, encouragement, and a great sense of friendship as we undertook this effort. He never took payment for his efforts on our behalf . . . and I still develop a lump in my throat when I remember that Leo passed away when he was not yet forty years old. A passing much too early in the face of the great, great future that should have been his!

In the very first days of its existence, the Institute had three rooms . . . three 1940 vintage Underwood manual typewriters, rented from an elderly gentleman, owner of the Rockefeller Center Typewriter Company . . . for the rental fee of $3.00 weekly per machine. Our typing classroom had three wooden tables and three folding chairs in addition to a blackboard donated by the same person who gave the tables. A desk for the office came from I no longer know where and, oh yes . . . we had the telephone . . . BR(yant) 9-0376!!!

And I hesitate to tell you how many times Dave or I went to the Whalen's Drug store to dial our number . . . and yes, we happily invested the five cents to know for sure that the phone was still in service.

And about the checking account. A business should have a checking account and Dave read in the newspaper . . . an ad . . . the New York Bank of Commerce was offering, free of charge, printed checks with name of business and address to companies that opened checking accounts with the Bank of Commerce. A good deal . . . and there was a branch on the northwest corner of 36th or 37th Street and 7th Avenue . . . and I went, in short order, to avail the Institute of the benefits being offered.

Upon entering the bank branch, I was directed to Mr. Shaw, the gentleman more than happy to assist me in my efforts to open a new business checking account . . . and oh, yes, the bank would supply checks printed at no charge in the name and address of the company:

Name of account: Spanish-American Institute
Address: 140 West 42 Street, New York, N.Y.
Owners: Frank J. Ferraro/David Schiffman

There were other questions: home addresses . . . age . . . places of employment . . . Social Security numbers, and whatever else. I answered the question and Mr. Shaw diligently recorded the information on the required bank forms. He had me sign on the proper line and gave me a signature card, which Dave should sign at the earliest so that the bank had available the signatures needed to conduct our financial transactions properly. Everything was quite clear and gathering up the forms, Mr. Shaw asked, "How much is your opening deposit?"

"Two hundred fifty dollars," I replied.

Mr. Shaw kind of slipped back into his chair. "We can't do that," he said very gently. "There's a minimum opening balance of $500 required for business checking accounts." Mr. Shaw was a great guy, but I only had $294 in my pocket. You may recall that our complete start-up capital was $500 and I had already paid Mr. Silverman $206.00 for March rent. There was no way this could happen today.

"I can't do that now, Mr. Shaw. I'm sorry." I looked squarely into Mr. Shaw's face. He really seemed like such a nice guy . . . "Mr. Shaw, can you hang on to those forms for a while? And as soon as I have the $500, I'll be back to open the account."

"I can do that," he said, as he placed the batch of forms into the bottom of his desk drawer. We shook hands and I left the bank and Mr. Shaw, fully expecting to return as soon as our economic situation permitted.

This banking situation took place in the first days of March 1955. I did return at a later date, and Mr. Shaw retrieved the application forms from his desk drawer. The account was opened with the required $500 deposit and the Institute, in short order received the promised quantity of "free" business checks. Mission accomplished.

We continued to use the Bank of Commerce branch until around 1970. It was our habit to make almost daily deposits to our account, and as the years went by, I was frequently greeted by Mr. Shaw. He was such a fine gentlemen . . . it even got to where he simply called me Frank . . . and that was how it went for all those years until one day . . . in 1970 . . . when Mr. Shaw invited me back to his desk.

"I want you to know," he said, "that I'm moving to our Bronx office. I'll be branch Vice President there." He seemed happy about that and then Mr. Shaw, looking directly at me: "You remember when we opened the account?" he asked.

I nodded. Of course, I remembered.

"Well, I want you to know," Mr. Shaw said, "that your school has become one of the most consistent regular daily deposit customers of this branch. It has been a real pleasure to know you. You've done a great job."

That was the last time I spoke to or saw Mr. Shaw . . . but the memory of his patient handling of our situation was etched in my consciousness: the manner in which a good businessman does his job to the benefit of all concerned.

The Institute remained at the 42nd Street address until early 1964. The enrollment grew from the original three students to a student body of thirty five, most of whom attended in the late afternoon and evening session. The school day was from 9:00 A.M. to 9:00 P.M. In July of 1955, the Institute was approved by the U.S. Department of Justice to enroll foreign students (with the I-20 Form), which permitted foreign students to enter the U.S. for educational purposes. This early approval was a most important element in the gradual but steady growth of the Institute. An insight into the make-up of the student body in these early formative years is, I think, of interest:

The largest group were of Puerto Rican origin. Their main goal was to improve their ability to speak, understand, read and write English. They usually attended in the evening session after a full day's work at what were most often minimum-wage jobs. They were a really exceptional group of young men and women (none below the age of seventeen) eager to learn . . . so eager, in fact, they paid their own tuition out of their modest weekly wages.

Then there were the Dominicans, who soon became a large segment of the student body . . . and we learned a bit about Rafael Trujillo.

As the years went by (through the late 50s), our enrollment required that the Institute expand . . . and so we did. We saw little of Mr. Silverman, and then we were notified that the building was sold to a Mr. Gaffney. We gradually expanded to all of the twelfth floor . . . then to the eleventh . . . and a bit later to the seventh and half of the sixth floor. Our typing room increased to include twenty-five rented Royal manuals . . . and our courses grew to include, in addition to English language, English and Spanish stenography, bookkeeping, import-export procedure, commercial correspondence, and advice on how to apply for employment: the application, résumé, the importance of personal appearance and the job interview. During this period, Dave supervised our employment placement program, which assisted our students in their efforts to find office employment.

There was also what was to become the beginning of the Spanish-American Institute bookstore . . . the main upshot of its beginning was the realization that in our dealings with the "newly arrived Americans," we could not expect that they knew their way around the city so well that they would easily find McGraw-Hill, Barnes & Noble or other carriers of the required texts.

It was also our way of ensuring that all students would be properly equipped with the texts, notebooks, pens, pencils, and other necessities of student life. It was, we felt, one small way of easing the student into a successful training experience and the hoped for office employment. Our experience, over time, convinced us that our students benefited from these conveniences, and the bookstore grew in proportion to the development of the Institute from year to year. And the student body continued to expand.

There were some from Argentina . . . and we heard about Peron and Peronistas . . . and then there were the Cubans and we learned a bit about Fulgencio Batista . . . the Tropicana . . . Varadero Beach . . . and later from a large segment of the dislodged Cuban middle class, we came to know, first hand, about Fidel Castro and Fidelistas. The Cuban students, like all of our students, were ambitious and eager to "make good" in their new land . . . and it was an absolutely great feeling, as a teacher, to be associated with so special a group of men and women.

Now I must take pause to name some outstanding people who came along in those earliest of days at the Institute. A young lady . . . Nola Serrano . . . who was employed in an office job but needed to brush-up in stenography. She enrolled for a brief period to increase her skills and in the process volunteered to teach two classes (evening session) of English and Spanish steno to beginners. She did this volunteer work for about two months . . . NO CHARGE . . . until she left in order to prepare for her upcoming marriage. This was such a great help to the Institute at that time. We did so very much appreciate it . . . our means were limited . . . our thanks sincere. We did manage to send a wedding gift . . . $50.00 . . . not much . . . but to this day we have never forgotten the helping hand extended by Nola Serrano.

There have been so very many unforgettable, unselfish, and giving people who contributed so very much to the development of the Institute: Aida Machado . . . Angela Almazan . . . Peter Delgado . . . Cesar Brenes . . . Ruth Zapata . . . Mrs. Moya . . . Miss Slocum . . . Mr. Perez . . . Segundo Aguinaga . . . Luisa Lahens . . . Dolores Abraham . . . and so very many others who gave their very best in service to the Institute. It is always less than wise to mention names . . . especially since there were so very many and omissions are almost inevitable . . . but in truth we have remained over the years eternally grateful to all who have in large or small measure assisted in the development of the Institute.

And Hyman G. Weiner, CPA. Hy Weiner, who came to us through one of Dave's brothers at a time when we were in dire need of financial guidance.

After the first six months of our "business life," we realized that an accountant was necessary to keep us abreast of city, state, and federal tax responsibility. So, in stepped Mr. Hyman G. Weiner, CPA, who remained with us for about thirty-eight years, until his passing. What an absolute asset Hy was to the Institute and our efforts! Not only in his capacity as our accountant, but as loyal and absolutely unselfish friend and advisor.

At first he came monthly . . . then as we grew, he came weekly and as time went on, he would spend two or three days of the week at the Institute attending to our increased accounting needs. Whatever, Hy was always there and the funny part was that although the workload grew larger . . . Hy NEVER increased his fee! It was only after we persisted and insisted that he accepted the slightest "salary" increase. No matter what I recall about Hy, it is impossible for me to express the appreciation, respect, and eternal love that I have felt for him and his humanity. His memory will live forever in me. He contributed so greatly to the development of the Institute and to my understanding of what TRUE friendship can mean in a lifetime.

2

As I indicated above, the Institute was steadily growing into the 1960s . . . and we were naturally adding faculty to cope with the increasing student body and increasing our subject matter effectiveness. There was a crying need for basic material in the teaching of English to the foreign born . . . and in our case especially to people of Spanish-speaking origin. This need gave birth to an English language workbook: "*Elementary English for Spanish-Speaking People,*" in 1957 . . . followed by "*Intermediate English for Spanish-Speaking People,*" and then "*Advanced English for the Foreign Born.*" I put together the first two workbooks and Dave the advanced level. They were registered with the Library of Congress and are used to this very day with additional material in our English-language classes.

It wasn't very long after the publication of the first workbook that I began to visualize the potential for English language records, which would make it possible for our students and otherwise interested persons to become familiar with and/or practice English at home or review lessons earlier presented in the classroom. It seemed logical that we could present the most basic core of the elementary workbook, which would offer an opportunity to carefully listen to and repeat vocabulary, common expressions, present-future-past tense of commonly used verbs, and a set of very basic questions and answers in addition to days of the week, months of the year, parts of the body, et. al.

I thought the "record set" should consist of forty lessons and provide a text wherein each page (divided down the middle) would provide in writing the spoken word presented on the record (left half of the page) and the Spanish meaning (right half of the page). It seemed to me that by giving the Spanish equivalent immediately, the student would spend little or no time translating and more time absorbing the verbal "music of the English language."

That was the plan. The idea seemed sound . . . but the economics . . . oh, well, there was just so much we could afford at that stage in our development, but . . .

I had a Webcor tape recorder at home. When I purchased it, the salesman at the Vim electronics department told me that it was the best of its kind on the market. It had served me very well, and so I started (at home during weekends) to formulate elementary English language lessons on tape . . . the hope that one day this material would be transferred to recordings and be available for use as outlined above.

This was a time-consuming and tedious undertaking. Not only was it necessary to repeat, correct, erase . . . repeat . . . pronounce and avoid the pitfalls of the "Brooklynese" that understandably crept into my effort . . . having been born, raised, and educated in that famous of all boroughs . . . but dealing with the constraints of time . . . having to present the lesson in a specific time frame that left one with the feeling that a particular linguistic goal was achieved.

The task was considerable and demanding for the above reasons in addition to the fact that the work area (in my home) had to be free of unexpected sounds, which when picked up by the recorder spoiled the lesson in progress, requiring erasure and the necessity to repeat the material. The most annoying obstacle in the home to the creation of an acceptable tape recording: the BASEMENT HEATING UNIT . . . in this case the oil burner! It would be off . . . quiet . . . and tape is rolling . . . and tape is rolling . . . quiet . . . and suddenly the start-up sound of the heating unit . . . the rattling noise ... STOP TAPE ... erase and re-tape as soon as the unit shuts off.

Solution: shut down the unit ... easy enough, weather permitting. In terms of the family: patience until the kids are off to bed ... and "thank you, dear wife, for postponing all kitchen sink and household cleaning activity until the taping session is over. Thank you."

In time and in this manner, believe it or not, there came the time when the forty lessons on tape were complete, intact, and ready for production when finances permitted. And in this regard, when the time was ripe, I was poised to meet with the Capitol Recording Company to advance the project as soon as the BUCKS were available.

Now why the Capitol Recording Company? The answer is quite simple: from as far back as I can remember, I was and have been an avid, loyal fan of Frank Sinatra ... and his earliest recordings were under the Capitol label. As an eighteen-year-old draftee serving in the 155 Field Artillery Battalion at Fort Sill, Oklahoma, and later in the ETO, I met a fellow draftee, Peter Leacock, an equally avid supporter of Dick Haymes. Our very frequent arguments re: Sinatra versus Haymes were constant and unending whenever we met ... though we always remained friends.

Many years later Peter Leacock became very well known as Peter Marshall, host of the popular "Hollywood Squares," a weekly TV show ... and still later a starring role on Broadway in *La Cage Aux Folles.* The theater was a few short blocks from the Institute, and I had the pleasure of meeting with him once or twice and visiting backstage when my family and I saw the show. By that time our discussions: Sinatra versus Haymes, had become somewhat of a mute point ... my Sinatra had unquestionably prevailed ... but running into Peter Marshall on several occasions over some forty years was always an absolute pleasure for me.

Let's face it: If Capitol Records were good enough for Sinatra, it was, without a doubt, the place for me! And so eventually with my Webcor forty-lesson elementary English tape in hand, I went to the Capitol Record studio ... around West 46th or 47th Street between 6th and 5th Avenue (as I recall) and presented my proposal for the production of English-language records by the Capitol Recording Company.

The individual with whom I spoke was very interested in my proposal, and he assured me that the Capitol recording facilities were available for projects along the lines that I had outlined. And when I told him about the many months I had spent producing the forty lessons perfectly on my Webcor recorder ... I thought the reproduction of the material from my tape to records would be a rather simple process. At that time he suggested that we play the tape to determine the time that would be required to present the forty-tape lessons on records ... and with this, my "perfect" tape was set into the studio play-back unit.

OH, MY GOODNESS!!! My perfect tape ... could this be possible? It had to be ... my own ears told me so. My voice was there ... the material was there ... but above it all was a steady, loud, unbroken screeching sound that made listening (to say nothing of understanding) for any length of time impossible.

I was amazed. The tape in my Webcor at home was, to coin a phrase, "as clean as a whistle" ... I didn't understand until it was explained to me that my tape was indeed perfect when produced and played on my unit at home ... but the super-sensitive professional studio equipment would reveal sounds not detected by a "general non-professional" recording unit.

We could still proceed with the project, but the material would have to be re-recorded in studio under the guidance of a sound engineer to assure the quality of the master from which many copies would be reproduced over time. The studio/engineer fee was set at $45 per hour, and the minimum record order was five-hundred copies. There would also be the design of record labels and the design/production of record jackets, which would be the Institute's responsibility. Naturally, the Institute would also provide the textbook that was to accompany the records to complete the set.

The plot had certainly thickened, but we were set to go . . . and so we went. The tape was timed at ninety minutes.

"How much studio/engineer time should we reserve?" the Capitol gentleman asked.

"Ninety minutes," my reply.

"You're gonna cut ninety minutes in ninety minutes?" Disbelief.

"I think so. I know the material. I've done it so many times."

"Well, okay . . . we'll set it up for ninety minutes and take it from there."

And so it was that two weeks later we re-recorded the material in studio . . . studio/engineer time ninety-three minutes. They were somewhat surprised . . . so much so that they did not charge the additional three minutes. The quality of their work was "A-One" as was their attention to our needs. We appreciated that.

In time the five-hundred copies of *"Ingles Elemental para Personas de Habla Castellana"* was delivered to the Institute. The forty basic lessons were presented on two 12-inch 33-1/3 speed records, which, except for a brief introduction in Spanish, utilized English only. At about the same time, we received the record jackets, which were designed by yours truly and printed by the dependable Dart Printing Company and George Goldie. It was on these record jackets that the Manhattan skyline, viewed from Weehawken or West New York, New Jersey, appeared as an Institute logo for the first time and for all the later years into the future.

With the receipt of this material, the Institute staff was immediately charged with the task of assembling records, sleeve, jacket and textbook to form the complete set ... readily available (price $7.95) in our bookstore and by mail order in response to ads in *El Diario* and *La Prensa*.

Production costs had consumed a considerable amount of our available resources, but it was our hope that sales, over time, would justify our initial outlay. There were two other record sets planned: the intermediate and advanced levels ... that would generally follow the elementary format, but present material graded to higher levels of proficiency. These projects were placed on hold in the light of our financial situation. The plans were there ... the time, who knew? And then ... who would believe?

3

It was mid-morning in the three-room twelfth-floor Spanish-American Institute when a middle-aged gentleman entered our space. He presented himself well and in acceptable English, with a trace of accent, asked if we had English-language records available for home study. Of course we did, and when he asked if he could listen to the material, of course he could. It was actually, in this instance, fortunate that we had no classes this early in the morning . . . an empty classroom provided privacy . . . and the visitor, seated at the teacher's table, had easy access to the record player that I carried into the room and plugged into the electric socket.

I placed lesson number one on the turntable . . . opened the text to the beginning, and closed the door behind me as I left the room. Except for the fact that I could hear my voice as the record proceeded from lesson to lesson, I could only assume that the visitor was attentive to the materials . . . and after more than an hour, he emerged from the classroom and took those dozen or so steps into my office.

"That was very good," he said. "They are very basic . . . very good for a beginner." And then, removing a kind of identification card from his pocket: "I am a representative of the Mexican Department of Education, Mexico City, D.F., and we are interested in records such as these for our students."

My head was swimming.

"I am authorized to place an order of up to one-thousand copies at the $7.95 price . . . but the jacket must show the price in pesos and there must be a notice (on the jacket) that the material contained is "approved by the

Department of Education, Mexico City, D.F." He also stipulated that the material was to be shipped directly to the Mexico City address that he provided within sixty days of the order.

We saw no problem meeting his requirements. The details were worked out . . . necessary agreements signed . . . 50 percent deposit paid with balance to follow delivery. Thus, the deal was closed.

And the activity of my next three days: contact Dart Printing to print one-thousand jackets (with necessary changes) and one-thousand texts. Send this material, ASAP, to indicated Mexico City address. Contact Capitol Records: produce one-thousand record sets and ship same, ASAP, to the indicated address. After a ten-day period . . . almost daily contact with the above companies to assure that we were on track. And finally, within the agreed time frame, the full delivery of the order and receipt of the balance due from Mexico City, D.F.

Who would believe? But that's the way it was and, oh, yes, suddenly we had the where-with-all to undertake the remainder of our project: *"Ingles Intermedio para Personas de Habla Castellana,"* by Frank J. Ferraro and *"Ingles Avanzado Para Personas de Habla Castellana,"* by David Schiffman.

The completion of our English-language record series, several years ahead of schedule, thanks to this heaven-sent stroke of good fortune . . . or was it that?

These materials were available to our students and in some instances were purchased from the Institute bookstore by individuals who had through family and/or friends heard of their home-study value. The language records were, from the outset, very popular . . . with the passage of time and improved technology, they were repackaged as cassettes and finally, to this day, in the form of CDs.

There were so many people so eager to offer a helping

hand to the Institute's mission. In retrospect I think that they felt a sense of satisfaction and pride in the knowledge that they were "lending a hand" in the development of an institution dedicated to the success and advancement of their community. There were so many people, but HOW DID WE GET THE WORLD-AT-LARGE to care for and know about the Spanish-American Institute?

In the beginning, when our resources were so very limited and really throughout the history of the Institute, "word of mouth and personal recommendation" were our best source of enrollments . . . although from the outset the Spanish language newspapers were in our affordability range and frequently used. Both *El Diario* and *La Prensa* (they were separate entities then) became our main sources of advertising . . . and believe me when I remember how helpful Darial Steer of *La Prensa* and Ruben Batista of *El Diario* were to us in our dealings with the education departments of their respective publications. We generally ran weekend ads and by skillfully pitting Steer against Batista, we often managed to receive "publicity articles" at no charge, except the promise of continued advertising in their weekly editions.

In the very late 50s, I made contact with radio station WWRL (I don't remember just how) to present a program each morning (at about 6:00 A.M.) of basic English for Spanish-speaking people. The program was not more than about fifteen minutes and presented as a public service by WWRL and the directors of the Spanish-American Institute.

I would go to the station offices (as I recall on the east side of 42nd Street) after 9:00 P.M. on Friday evenings and tape the five lessons that would be presented on air at about 6:00 A.M. of the following five weekday mornings. These "at no cost spots" were very helpful, especially when I convinced Ruben Batista that there should be a public service column in *El Diario,* which presented English language lessons to its readers in conjunction with the directors of the Spanish-American Institute. These were the early advertising assets that we had, and they were enough together with the expanding needs of the Spanish-speaking community to enhance our growth as an educational institution.

From the beginning, 1955 to 1962, the Institute was a "handshake partnership" between Frank and Dave, but in 1962 at the behest of Hy Weiner and the legal advice of Leo Darzy, a corporation was formed: Frank J. Ferraro, Pres./Treas. And David Schiffman, V.P./Sec. All things were on a really GREAT track . . . right through the early 60s . . . everyone and everything just FANTASTIC . . . until one morning in 1964 . . . I arrived as usual to our twelfth floor offices and BANG!!!

What news? Who would believe? The look of despair on Aida Machado's face . . . our receptionist, told it all . . . in addition to the wide yellow tape that lined the entrance to the office: Fire Hazard . . . Do not enter . . . Fire Dept. City of New York.

When I met with the fire chief, I was advised that we must vacate the building POST HASTE!! The building was not suitable for public assembly. The stairway was too narrow . . . the elevators inadequate . . . there were no fire escapes . . . no sprinkler systems . . . and the size of our student body too large for the locale . . . inadequate bathrooms . . . we must vacate POST HASTE!!!

The students. What to do with our students?

I don't remember exactly how, but I came to know that a lawyer, David Goldstick, was somehow the Democrat leader or part of the leadership of the Time Square (or 42nd Street) area. He had offices in the French Building, around 43rd or 44th Street and Fifth Avenue . . . a short walk from where we were, and so I went . . . POST HASTE . . . to ask for help from Mr. David Goldstick, attorney-at-law.

The French Building was very impressive. Beautiful lobby . . . spacious elevators . . . uniformed attendants. And entering the law offices of I don't remember the first name, Alperstein and Goldstick, I was very promptly admitted into the office of Mr. Goldstick . . . a younger man than I might have expected . . . very friendly . . . quick speaking . . . but a very good listener.

I introduced myself, and as briefly as I could explain this very serious situation to Mr. Goldstick . . . vacate POST HASTE!! But my students . . . what could I do about my students? He listened very attentively, then asked several necessary questions:

The name of the school. How long at the 42nd Street address? Name and address of the owners. How many students. Teachers.

Were there any particular problems with the Institute?

Mr. Goldstick made quick notes of the information . . . then "I'll see what, if anything, can be done," Mr. Goldstick said. "I'll get back to you as soon as I can," he concluded with a shake of my hand. "Sit tight," he said finally as I left the office. . . . "Let's see what cooks."

I was numb with fear. We had lived through the anxiety of the Bay of Pigs invasion . . . the assassination of JFK . . . and who knows what else? But now . . . this was the limit!

How long? I could not believe when the phone rang the very next day . . . early in the morning. It was David Goldstick . . . Mr. David Goldstick . . .

"Good morning, Frank. I spoke with the office of Mayor Robert Wagner . . . and the mayor has issued a stay of the order to vacate. You may continue at 140 West 42nd Street for the next thirty days . . . but no more than that, Frank . . . do you understand?"

"Oh, yes, I do, Mr. Goldstick. Thank you so very much. You've been just great," I continued, "I don't know how to thank you enough."

"It's quite all right," Goldstick said as the phone conversation ended. "Remember, Frank . . . thirty days . . . and good luck."

A thirty-day stay of the vacate order. How absolutely wonderful. That Goldstick was an absolute angel. Thirty days to continue normally at 140 West 42nd Street . . . a Godsend . . . but then . . .

What . . . how . . . when . . . and most of all WHERE TO???

4

LOCATION . . . Location . . . location
THE NEXT MOVE
1964

The thirty-day stay of the order to vacate was the lifting of a great sense of anxiety from our shoulders . . . to be sure . . . but the sense of relief was quickly removed by the realization that we had to find new quarters as soon as possible . . . but where to?

And so the search was begun . . . at first with references to the real estate pages of every New York City newspaper. A good lead in the 34th Street and 7th Avenue area turned out to be out of our "desired area" . . . too many large department stores: Macy's, Gimble's . . . Madison Square Garden . . . too much all-direction traffic . . . but more to the point, nothing seemed to meet our desire for an adequate school space . . . easily accessible to our students.

Then the search in the low 40s . . . a promising space on 40th Street between 5th and 6th Avenue. Not a bad space, but not for us in the end . . . too off Broadway and the West Side subway exits. And then Bryant Park and the Public Library . . . our students would have to walk quite a bit from west side subway exits or several long blocks from Port Authority Bus Terminal. The need for them to make their way around the park was of concern to us, so that we turned our search to the mid-40s from 6th Avenue to 8th Avenue . . . and having exhausted the newspaper ads, I began again to search on foot . . . block by block and building by building. We had a stay of thirty days, but after the first week, I knew that the resolution would not come easily . . . but the search continued.

Whatever else was lacking in the Times Square area of the 60s, there was no shortage of theaters, movie houses, porno shops, and restaurants. Looking east, on the south side of 42nd Street beyond the porno theater about mid-way up the block, was the 42nd Street Cafeteria, and just north of it a good-sized office building—no space available—and across 6th Avenue looking toward 5th Avenue, Bryant Park and the New York Public Library. All very well, but no space for a school there!

On 42nd Street looking west toward 6th Avenue was Stern's Department store and a large Woolworth Five and Dime . . . and below 6th Avenue looking toward Broadway on the south side of 42nd Street . . . a series of street-level shops selling everything from used books and magazines to cheap jewelry and souvenirs in addition to several more porno shops. Above these shops were usually one or two floors of space devoted to employment placement offices, a private detective agency, a fortune teller's tea room, and a private check-cashing service. None of these areas offered an adequate amount of space to say nothing about the lack of eye appeal. And so we traveled west on 42nd Street to Broadway looking toward 8th Avenue.

On the corner of 42nd Street and Broadway stood the much-frequented Whalen's Drug Store . . . a really popular spot not only for its long soda fountain service counter and delicious cakes, pies, soda, ice cream, coffee, tea and whatever else one might fancy on the run . . . all of which available twenty-four hours daily . . . but for the "actor and actress" hopefuls happily employed there to be close to and available for the big show-biz break and a shot at stardom that they hoped would come their way.

This Whalen's Drug Store had been a frequent stop, so

nearby to the school since 1955 . . . but now, standing on this corner looking west on 42nd Street toward 8th Avenue and walking both sides of the street, which were overflowing with X-rated movie houses on either side, more porno shops, quick-stop hot dog and soda shops, in addition to several cigarette, newspaper, and candy stores—nothing there suitable for the Institute.

And so we continued our search up Broadway, looking uptown beyond the internationally famous Times Tower, set atop the triangle that divides Broadway and Seventh Avenue to downtown traffic, at the same time that it flashes the latest world headlines to the thousands who daily, for business or pleasure, traverse the busy streets of mid-town Manhattan.

On the Tuesday of the second week of our plan to search out every street north from 42nd to 50th . . . 6th Avenue to 8th Avenue east and west was resumed at 44th Street going west toward 8th Avenue. On the south side, the rear platform loading areas of the *New York Times* . . . which took about half the block . . . then the famous Sardi's . . . followed by several rehearsal stages and one or two popular Broadway theaters. On the north side of 44th Street, the Shubert Theater . . . Shubert Alley . . . several restaurants . . . absolutely wonderful, but . . . nothing here for us.

I began to make my way east on 44th Street and about one-third the way up the block from Broadway, on the north side: Lucca's Italian Restaurant. I had on more than several occasions enjoyed lunch at Lucca's . . . a clean, family-owned-and-operated establishment . . . delicious veal cutlet parmigiana, including a side order of spaghetti, a slice or two of warm bread, and maybe a beer or soda . . . all served in an atmosphere of friendship and, as I recall, priced under $3.00!!

And so with these pleasant thoughts in mind, I decided

to stop in for some delicious Italian food, after which I had every intention . . . with renewed vigor . . . to continue the search.

The restaurant had seating at tables for at best thirty-six to forty diners, but in mid-afternoon, after the lunch hours and before dinner time, seating was no problem. I readily found my place at table, placed my order with the waitress, and in a very short time began to savor my favorite dish amid the pleasant atmosphere of Lucca's Italian Restaurant.

When I had just about completed my dinner, Mr. Lucca, as was his custom, entered the dining room from the kitchen area walking toward my table, a warm friendly smile on his face . . . his hand extended for handshake: "Mr. Frank," his greeting. "How've you been? You look just great . . . and how goes the Institute?"

"Pretty good," I responded . . . but then without hesitation, I found myself telling him about our need to find new quarters . . . the POST HASTE order of the Fire Department . . . the subsequent thirty-day stay of the order, and my inability, thus far, to find suitable space in the Times Square area. And, of course, I was anxious about the need to relocate our student body with the very least possible upset. We were doing very well "student population" wise . . . and, of course, I was very concerned . . . and Mr. Lucca was perhaps exactly what I needed at this time . . . I think it did me some good to "talk out" some of my anxiety . . . but not nearly as much good as what Mr. Lucca was about to suggest: "Have you ever been to the Hotel King Edward?" he asked.

"No."

"Well," he continued, "I don't know if anything can come of it . . . but the owner of the hotel, Miss Candia, is a regular with me."

With this Mr. Lucca pointed toward a table in the far corner of the room . . . and then I noticed a placard:

RESERVED . . . set in the middle of the table. "She is with us for dinner three or four times a week, usually later in the evening, sometimes alone, but oftentimes with three or four associates or friends."

Mr. Lucca then told me that Miss Candia had recently mentioned her intention to make some modifications in the organization of the hotel. He didn't know the details, but he knew that she was seeking to increase the occupancy rate, which had fallen below desirable levels . . . competition from new hotels and the sluggish economy together with a slump in tourism were taking its toll.

"Why don't you stop in?" Mr. Lucca suggested. "It's only up the street . . . 120 West 44th . . . you can mention to Miss Candia that I thought she might be interested . . . and that there may be something there for both of you."

I thanked Mr. Lucca for this information and assured him that my next stop on this very day would be at 120 West 44th Street . . . the Hotel King Edward . . . and a meeting, I hoped, with this lady: Miss Candia.

How odd it was that in the normal order of things the next area in my "street search" before I decided to break for lunch, was 44th Street from Broadway to Sixth Avenue.

I lost no time making my way to the Hotel King Edward on the south side of 44th Street . . . the double glass door entrance opened to a modestly decorated, sparsely furnished lobby to the right of which was a long reception counter . . . behind which stood the hotel desk clerk.

"Good afternoon, may I help you?"

"Yes, thank you. Is Miss Candia available?"

"She's in the building. Is she expecting you?"

"Not really . . . she's been recommended to me by a mutual friend . . . and if she has the time . . ."

The desk clerk quickly punched out three or four numbers as she raised the telephone to her ear . . . and in the next second: "There's a gentleman to see you," and after a pause . . . "Okay."

In almost no time at all a well-dressed, middle-aged woman stepped through the doorway of an office area situated behind and to the left of the reception counter.

"Yes, sir . . . may I help you?" Her manner very friendly and on that note, I briefly outlined my need for office space and Mr. Lucca's suggestion that maybe she . . . Miss Candia . . . might be of help. I made her aware of the Institute . . . that we were located on 42nd Street since 1955 . . . that things were going well for us, but our need to vacate our present space was by order of the New York City Fire Department . . . hence our need to find suitable space as soon as possible.

For her part Miss Candia explained that she was in the process of reorganizing the use of space available in the building. It was her intention to find long-term tenants for the lower three floors of the building while continuing to function as a tourist/visitor hotel facility on the upper stories. She noted that space had already been leased to a chiropractor, a dentist, a medical doctor, and an osteopath . . . and she expressed the hope that perhaps we might be able to work something out to our mutual advantage. This conversation resulted in a tour of the available space and eventually led to a nearly perfect arrangement for the hotel and the Institute.

At the north end of the lobby was a large ballroom area—now vacant . . . an excellent space for our "machine room" . . . just great for our typing and machine transcription classes.

Above the lobby was a large mezzanine area consisting of five rooms . . . very suitable for classrooms . . . and a suite of three rooms to be used as offices and a modest bookstore facility. And best of all, perhaps, the fact that all rooms were served by a common hallway with separate entrances that preserved the privacy of each unit at the same time assuring the free flow of traffic.

The mezzanine area was accessible by two wide stairways, making it completely unnecessary for our students to use the elevators. Our occupancy of the street level, off the lobby area, "machine room" and the mezzanine would keep us comfortably apart from hotel-guest traffic.

The situation looked promising, and on that basis, further meetings were held, terminating in a five-year lease agreement and the Institute's plan to move into the new address ASAP!!

In all our planning and discussions regarding a new location, we had never considered hotel space, and yet in retrospect, such space offered more than a few vitally important features, basic to a school's occupancy, which we, as ambitious but inexperienced individuals, had been completely unaware of in 1955 when we established the Institute.

For example: we would now be occupying a building that had a certificate of occupancy permitting public assembly. It contained approved fire-alarm systems and multiple means of egress. Each classroom had its own bathroom facility, and the building provided heat and air conditioning. The hotel housekeeping unit was responsible for the cleanliness of our areas, including the vacuuming of floors and the washing of windows. These tasks were attended to overnight, after school closing at 9:00 P.M.

5

All in all, there were positives resulting from the need to move . . . at the same time, a touch of sadness in leaving our "first home," which, after all, was the site of our birth.

Then with the excitement of a "new home" pounding in our chests, we drove into the heavy-duty-full-speed-ahead activity of the next fifteen days.

It goes without saying that classes were going on as usual during our "search period," and we were careful that our moving would in no way interfere with our attention to students. Our dedicated faculty and efficient office staff, small in number though they were, deserved the highest praise for their efforts . . . and once we knew that "moving day" was fifteen days hence, we settled into directly coping with the problems of the "BIG MOVE" . . . and there were more than a few.

We started by designating each classroom in the new facility with a room number . . . and then we tagged each item of furniture in the old facility so that upon moving from the "old," it would be placed in the designated room number of the "new." Typewriters, typewriter tables, folding chairs, two portable blackboards . . . to the "machine room" with two teacher's desks.

Student tablet-arm chairs, about forty of them, tagged with the "new" room number so that about eight of them would be placed therein together with the necessary blackboard, teacher's desk, and two folding chairs. Textbooks were boxed and bookcases tagged for proper placement in the "new" bookstore . . . and student records, file cabinets, carbon copying machine, stationery, etc., were earmarked "office."

With all this activity in addition to the normal classroom schedule, I think the saving grace was that although the student body had grown steadily since 1955, the growth was mostly from 4:00 to 9:00 P.M., the vast majority attending after their full-time work day. There was also class-size growth from 9:00 A.M. to 12 noon . . . generally young men and women not engaged in early morning employment, or attending under the I-20 foreign student program.

The afternoon hours, generally from about 12 noon to 4:00 P.M. were open except for "private students" who desired "one on one" English language instruction. These private students were usually older professionals, well-educated quick learners, and a good source of tuition income, since the hourly rate for private sessions was more expensive than that of group classes.

All in all these pre-move days were busy indeed and as we drew closer to "moving day," we made a tour of the new facility with faculty and staff, after which we instructed our students as to their classroom assignments and room numbers at our new address: 120 West 44th Street . . . a few steps east of Times Square!

Now there was a three-day weekend coming up . . . I don't remember if in May or July . . . nevertheless, our plan was to hold regular classes to 9:00 P.M. Friday evening in the "old" facility . . . move everything to 44th Street by Saturday evening . . . make everything presentable over Sunday and Monday (the holiday) . . . in order to welcome our students to their NEW Spanish-American Institute on Tuesday, A.M.

That was the plan, and with the help of our faculty, the office staff in addition to family, a few friends and several student volunteers, the plan was implemented successfully and on schedule.

Setting into the new facility was easier than we had anticipated. Having all classrooms, bookstore, and offices on one level (the mezzanine) was an improvement from the three floors previous required . . . and the "machine room" at the north end of the lobby (once the main ballroom) made the housing of all typewriters in one area very comfortable, still leaving room for a section devoted to English and Spanish steno transcription classes. The hotel staff from Miss Candia to her associates, the housekeeping and custodial crew, were pleasantly friendly and most helpful in their dealings with us, and we were most appreciative of their efforts.

In the ensuing months, we purchased additional tablet armchairs to accommodate our desired class size of no more than twelve students. Our school day remained 9:00 A.M. to 9:00 P.M., five days weekly. We discontinued our typewriter rental service and purchased thirty new Royal manuals. This purchase marked the first time in our business life that we entered into a "loan agreement" . . . we paid "X" dollars up front with the balance due in monthly payments over three years. Several of our part-time faculty were able to increase their hours at the same time that new hires were added as office aides and bookstore clerks. The Institute had settled in, and we were growing.

We continued our newspaper advertising in *El Diario/La Prensa* and selected Spanish-language magazines . . . at the same time that we added regular commercials on local radio stations: WADO . . . WWRL . . . WPOW and WHOM. This was a giant new step for the Institute, and thankfully positive results were immediate. At the outset we worked directly with the radio station: prepared the copy, selected air times, paid the ad fee in advance as required, and made efforts to monitor our "spot" when it came on.

This was our "modus operandi" until it was suggested to us by one of the station directors that it might well be in our best interest to engage an advertising agency. Such an agency might (if strong enough) command more favorable rates, especially when "economy package rates" were available. An agency would also monitor station broadcasting logs and win concessions when errors or omissions occurred. These suggestions seemed to make sense, and our brief search led us to Mr. Shalom Rubinstein and the Advertiser's Broadcasting Company . . . an organization well known and respected in the area of foreign language radio broadcasting. And what a really great choice it was . . . a relationship born in early 1965 and continued to the late 1980s, to the definite benefit of the Institute and its founders. An advantage most directly related to the exceptional character that was Shalom Rubinstein and his unselfish dedication to the continued growth and success of the Institute.

At the outset, our radio ad copy was delivered on air by station staff, but in time we took to recording ad copy in the offices of Shalom's Advertiser's Broadcasting Company . . . the tapes then forwarded to radio stations for broadcast. Our spots were generally 6:00 A.M. to 7:30 A.M. and in the evenings from 6:30 to 8:00 P.M., with an assortment of spots aired in afternoon hours affording the Institute the benefit of "economy package rates."

We always kept careful data re: the source of registrations . . . print media, radio advertising, recommendations (and later) TV. From the outset, no matter the totals, personal recommendations came up as the main source of student enrollments. A source of satisfaction to us because it meant that our faculty, office staff, directors, and the overall view of the Institute was positive in the minds of those who knew us best through personal and daily contact . . . to the extent that they would recommend us to friends, family, and folks they met at work and in day-to-day contacts.

It was my feeling that the radio and print media served

to introduce the public-at-large to the Institute . . . and that each registration resulting there from served as a "seed," which when properly cultivated led to the "word of mouth" that attracted a wider circle of students to the offerings of the school. Over the years hundreds of students became a part of our lives, as we have, hopefully, contributed to theirs. Impossible as it is to remember each individually, some remain forever in memory:

There were three sisters from Puerto Rico who had enjoyed some measure of popularity for their singing voices there under the name of "Las Hermanas Cabezudo." In addition to their study of the English language, they frequently entertained to the delight of our student body and friends at school dances and at times, we were told, in the homes of fellow students.

At another time, a well-dressed, intelligent, fairly well spoken gentleman attended daily private afternoon English language classes. He spoke English fairly well but wanted to expand his vocabulary and fluency. He was especially interested in hearing and learning expressions that native Americans (as he put it) used in everyday life. As a member of the Colombian delegation to the United Nations, and a member (through marriage) of the family of Rojas Pinilla, the ruler of Columbia, it was his desire to serve his position well and to interact comfortably with those with whom he had dealings, professionally in his work and socially in his relationships at the United Nations.

He was an ideal student . . . a solid educational background, multi-lingual, eager to learn, and with an excellent memory and a keen ability to grasp the material of the day. Our sessions were "one on one," and gradually over many weeks, we developed a friendly sense of mutual respect . . . so much so that he invited me to relocate to Bogota for the purpose of establishing a government-sponsored English language school. He knew that I was married with two children and assured me that his government would provide airline transportation for me and my family, housing in Bogota, a generous wage, an automobile and housekeeping services to assist my wife.

His proposal was sincere and I was pleased that he would think so well of me . . . but as respectfully as I knew how, I thanked him for the offer . . . but such a relocation was impossible due to my commitments to the Spanish-American Institute. He was very understanding of my situation, and our friendly relationship continued to term's end. In time the regime of Rojas Pinilla ended, and with it I assume, a change in the make-up of the Colombian delegation to the United Nations.

In the early 60s, with Fidel Castro in control of Cuba, we were stunned at the Institute when we received an invitation on the letterhead of the Cuban Ministry of Education, signed by Che Guevara (as Minister of Education) to visit the island at our convenience to undertake a study of the island's school system. It was a very flattering invitation, but I instinctively knew would likely never come to pass.

As a matter of fact, political events evolved so rapidly that I knew "this trip" would NEVER come to pass . . . and so I took the letter and attached it to the back of one of the picture frames that adorned the walls of our reception area. The months and years went by . . . we were more than occupied with our daily routines and on the few occasions that I remembered the letter, my efforts to find it never bore fruit . . . and to this day I know not behind which picture frame it was or is or where it went.

At the Institute we received anti-Batista Cuban exiles through the 50s and anti-Castro exiles through the mid- and late 60s . . . and a cardinal class rule throughout the Institute was "no politics, religion, or personal attacks" . . . we are all family here.

Happily, the atmosphere was almost always friendly, respectful, and conducive to learning. Our students were all seventeen years of age or older. They attended of their own volition, paid tuition, which in many instances represented a meaningful expense relative to their income. They were quite serious in their studies . . . they had vital goals in mind, which would have an impact on the quality of their lives in their new world. There were so very many good people from so many different places . . . many of them etched forever in my mind for one reason or another . . . and among the most memorable were Maria Brenes and Lilia Lazo, both aspiring actresses who had enjoyed a measure of success in Cuba . . . careers interrupted by the political upheaval there . . . but now (in the U.S.A.) hopeful that they could resume their dreams in spite of their problem . . . the English language . . . hence, the Spanish-American Institute.

Maria Brenes, the older of the two (I was told), had enjoyed considerable success in Cuba, while Lilia had barely begun to enjoy some recognition as a comedian. They attended semi-private classes together for a time, after which they continued classes in evening session groups. After a time Lilia's husband opened a Spanish-style restaurant, uptown in the city, and she was, naturally, helping him in his efforts. I heard little else about Lilia or Maria for about two years when our paths again crossed.

There were also the three brothers, from about eight to twelve years of age—the sons of a general high up in the government of Venezuela, who, as the story was related to me, conspired with two other Army generals to overthrow the reigning dictator. The attempt was successful when the general's shots hit their mark. The victim fell dead, whereupon two of the generals immediately assassinated the third general (father of the boys) and assumed control of the government.

The three boys and their widowed mother were provided passage to the U.S. where they were placed in housing and awarded a monthly monetary allowance from the government of Venezuela. The three brothers were enrolled at the Institute for about two months (during the summer, when regular school was closed for vacation) in a semi-private class, which met daily for one hour. We never met their mother, but each afternoon a limo (delegate plates) pulled up to curbside at the Institute. The driver remained with the vehicle while a gentleman accompanied the boys to their English class. He remained outside but near to the classroom door until the session ended, and he escorted them back to the limo and home, wherever that was.

The boys were very well behaved, and their progress with us seemed satisfactory although it was obvious that they had received previous English language training and I was sure they would continue their schooling with the opening of the regular school year. The gentleman guardian was always proper though almost never very talkative. But over the weeks that we were exposed to each other, he gradually relaxed and revealed the events that I have outlined above. With summer's end came the end of my contact with the boys . . . and over the years I have from time to time wondered where they are and how they are now.

We were always aware that our effectiveness as a school was directly related to best serving the needs of our students, but we wanted also to be approved, accredited, certified (and whatever else positive) in the eyes of the community-at-large. We were members in good standing of the Better Business Bureau, and we were since 1955 authorized under federal law to enroll non-immigrant foreign students. But we thought there should be more and I contacted the

Board of Education at 110 Livingston Street, Brooklyn. When our inquiries went unanswered, I contacted the New York State Department of Education, Albany, New York. They notified us that as we were a private school serving students seventeen years of age and older, their department had no jurisdiction.

I was aware that in the early 50s the Eisenhower administration established the Department of Health, Education and Welfare . . . hence I sent inquiries to that agency, hoping that approval from this federal department would offer certification or accreditation status and enhance our standing in the eyes of the community-at-large . . . but my correspondence was met with silence.

At the Institute we had developed our own "in house system" of checks and balances. Dave held monthly group teacher meetings in which general schoolwide matters were discussed. He also scheduled regular weekly meetings with faculty, "one on one," to cope with specific classroom situations: course material and coverage, effective use of textbooks, homework assignments, exam schedules, grades, student progress and attendance. He was also "the tracker" of tuition payments, and when necessary the contact with individuals in tuition arrears.

6

Both Frank and Dave made it a practice to "sit in" on classes to personally observe student participation and progress. These "sit-ins" depended on the constraints of time and as other duties permitted . . . but they never occurred without prior notice to the faculty member. These classroom visits were generally well received . . . giving the directors the opportunity to observe and evaluate class activity in real time while giving the students and faculty the feeling that their performances were important to the directors.

We were doing such things as these, but it seemed that there should be an agency of government to which we could submit our credentials, so to speak . . . an agency that would perform objective oversight . . . that would review our methods, evaluate our efforts, and hopefully accredit, verify, validate, certify (and whatever else) our existence to the community-at-large.

While this was not the case, we carved our own path as best we knew how . . . moving forward in terms of student population growth . . . course and curriculum development . . . faculty expansion . . . textbook and technology development. And at that point in time, all was well.

Then one afternoon (I think around 1958) there was a telephone call at the Institute from the office of the Federal Department of Education, Washington, D.C., I was notified that a Mr. Allen (as I recall the name) would be attending conferences in New York City during the upcoming week and that he would be able to visit the Institute on Friday afternoon, if we were available. The visit was to be informal and subject to change if unexpected conditions altered Mr. Allen's schedule.

WOW . . . of course we were available, and thank you.

On that Friday afternoon, Mr. Allen appeared as planned. A tall, well-spoken gentleman who extended his hand in a friendly handshake and gave the impression during his entire two-hour visit that his stop was not only informal but somehow an interesting personal side trip of his own choosing. He asked a few questions as we began our conversation, which led to information re: our birth as an institute . . . a brief sketch of the directors as founders . . . the faculty . . . a profile of our student body, curriculum, textbooks and a tour (as we spoke) of the office, classrooms and bookstore. Remember in 1958 we were at the 42nd Street address . . . the facilities quite simple and easy to encapsulate. He did not ask to interview faculty or students, but I felt certain he had a sense of the general atmosphere as he toured our rather uncomplicated facility.

Mr. Allen's visit, informal, to be sure, was for me a very important event in the short lifetime of the Institute. And when he indicated that it was time to make his way to Penn Station and his train ride back to D.C., I felt that a friend was about to take his leave. I thanked him for his visit as we paused briefly on the downtown side of Broadway. Mr. Allen took my hand in a friendly handshake . . . then in words I have never forgotten:

"You have a very good thing going here," he said. "Keep doing what you are doing . . . develop it . . . expand it to the very best of your ability" . . . and then after a pause . . . "and don't worry about approvals, government agencies and certifications . . . if you develop seriously and well, these agencies will eventually seek you out and recognize your efforts."

Again I thanked him for his visit and his kind words. A cab pulled up to curbside where we stood . . . Mr. Allen stepped in . . . the cab door slammed shut and in the very few next moments was swallowed up in traffic on the way to Penn Station and the train to D.C.

In the many years since Mr. Allen's visit, I have always cherished the memory of our meeting . . . but it was not until about fifteen years later that I realized the prophetic accuracy of the advice he extended personally to me as we parted company forever on that Friday afternoon in the late 1950s.

By 1965 we had settled comfortably into our Hotel King Edward facility, and for the first time, we undertook the airing of a schedule of commercials on Spanish language TV: Channel 47 and somewhat later Channel 41. As closely as we had been working with Shalom Rubenstein in the planning and presentation of radio ads . . . the world of TV advertising required not only the careful preparation of the message but an ability to coordinate the message with effective visual images that would accurately portray the Institute and its educational mission to the community it served. This photographic "know-how" was provided by Lew Merrim, who had for many years worked hand-in-hand with Shalom . . . and Lew's ability with the camera quickly became an immediate asset to our TV efforts.

At first the presentations were quite simple and direct utilizing the "talking head" of Frank J. Ferraro, founder and president of the Spanish-American Institute, inviting the viewer to contact the Institute for English language courses and/or training in secretarial and business studies leading to higher paying office employment.

The typical English language course commercial:

Si ud. Quiere aprender Ingles	If you would like to learn English
escribirlo bien,	write well,
entenderlo mejor,	understand better,

visitenos en el	visit us at the
Spanish-American Institute	Spanish-American Institute
120 Calle Oeste 44	120 West 44th Street
en Times Square	in Times Square
clases en conversacion,	classes in conversation,
gramatica y escritura	grammar and writing
bajo direccion de	under the direction of
profesores universitarios	university professors
dedicado a su exito.	dedicated to your success.
clases disponible durante	classes available during
el dia o de noche.	day or evening sessions.
Visitenos en el	Visit us at the
Spanish-American Institute	Spanish-American Institute
120 calle oeste 44	120 West 44th Street
en Nueva York . . . o para	in New York . . . or for
mas informacion	more information
Telefono BR 9-0376	Telephone BR 9-0376
Su futuro le espera!	Your future awaits you!

Our TV commercial: preparation for office employment followed a very similar approach . . . again using the "talking head" to outline the availability of courses in stenography, typing, bookkeeping, office practice, import-export procedure . . . and the hope that such training would lead to better paying office employment. Our closing line in almost every commercial: *en el Spanish-American Institute . . . su futoro le esperá!* (Your future awaits you at the Spanish-American Institute!)

The commercials appeared regularly during evening hours; their effectiveness evident by the increase in telephone inquiries and personal visits in addition to increased enrollments in all courses of study. And there was another interesting (though unexpected) result of our TV commercials:

It happened the first time one day when I passed through the reception area. Several young men and women were awaiting their interview turn with one of our office staff. As I walked by . . . "He's on TV," whispered one to the other . . . "I saw him on TV."

After that first time, it happened often in the school, and I adjusted to my newly found "fame." It was, on further thought, to be expected on Institute grounds . . . but then another "unexpected" situation arose when I stopped into a Ray's Pizza Parlor for a quick lunch and one of the servers told his work partner: "This guy's on TV *el habla espanol.*" (he speaks Spanish). I nodded "yes" . . . took my slice of pizza to a quiet spot at the stand-up customer-eating counter.

And then my "A" train subway ride from 178th Street to 42nd Street in the A.M. and my return in the evening. On the platform at 42nd Street, a friendly, smiling face: "I seen you on TV. Spanish-American school . . . *habla Espanol?*"

I returned the friendly smile, *"Si, señor. Gracias."* The "A" train pulled into the station. The doors slid open . . . I entered . . . found my seat and *Wow, those ads are really working.* I thought . . . *and thank you much for that, Shalom.*

About once a month, we would meet at the TV studio to redo and freshen our commercials . . . Shalom, Lew Merrim, and myself . . . usually in a historical landmark theater in Newark, and less frequently in Secaucus, New Jersey. Lew took some effective still photos of students and teachers in classroom situations so that after our "talking head" intro, the visuals would switch to the still photos depicting a typing class and/or a group of steno students: steno pads and pencils at the "dictation ready" while the voice-over described the activity . . . gave the address . . . phone number . . . and invited the viewer to visit or contact the Spanish-American Institute for further information.

It was during one of these studio sessions that because

of some in-house problem, there was a delay in the availability of facilities and I was asked to wait in a studio anteroom while Shalom and Lew worked out whatever the "kinks" were. In the same waiting room was a very well-dressed gentleman who introduced himself ... "Carlos Montalban" ... and then a broad smile lighting every inch of his face.... "El Exigente." And then I knew ... of course ... Mr. Colombian Coffee. He was accompanied by his wife, who was thoroughly involved in the care of her three meticulously combed, manicured, and groomed toy poodles ... ribbons, bows and all.

Mr. Montalban was very proud of his "Exigente character" and the fact that his commercial was so frequently aired and in so very many TV markets. He informed me that he earned $59 in residual fees for each time the commercial aired. He further informed me that his brother, Ricardo Montalban, was an actor in Hollywood and then ... his broad smile again in full bloom ... he told me that he (Carlos) made more money as "El Exigente" than his brother, Ricardo, earned in his entire Hollywood acting career. He did not relate this information with any air of "bragadoccio" ... but simply as friendly conversation with only perhaps the gentlest touch of sibling rivalry. Although I accepted his assessment as accurate at the time, I became aware some years later, that Ricardo's role in "Fantasy Island" (big TV hit) in addition to other motion picture successes must have bested the earning power of "El Exigente."

At another time I was invited to participate in a panel discussion with three fellow panelists ... one of them a young political activist ... Herman Badillo ... where we exchanged ideas and our observations regarding the efforts of Hispanics to prosper and succeed in their new environment. Mr. Badillo's sincerity and dedication to the community he served was admirable as was, over the many years later, his contributions and service to the people of the city of New York.

Some years later I served on a panel of judges in a beauty contest on Channel 47, which required my appearance one evening a week for one month of the contest's duration. These were wonderful opportunities to present the Institute, which was always mentioned together with its founder and director. Valuable exposure at no cost beyond our time . . . exposure which certainly expanded the community's awareness of the Institute and its work. We offered a six-month Secretarial or English language course as one of the prizes available to the winner.

We came to realize how popular this type of contest was . . . so much so that each year at the Institute, the students selected (by secret ballot) "Miss Spanish-American Institute" who was presented with her court of attendants and crowned at our graduation exercises, which included a dinner dance . . . very well attended by graduates, family and friends, in addition to faculty, office staff, and current students. Newspaper coverage of these events always followed . . . reminders to the Hispanic community of the Institute and the educational service it provided.

And then there was Lilia Lazo. The aspiring young actress who upon her arrival from Cuba attended English language classes at the Institute in the hope that she might resume her career in her new country. Several years had passed since our last contact, but we were aware that Lilia was appearing weekly on Spanish language TV . . . in a comedic sitcom . . . *Popa En Nueva York* . . . that had become one of the more popular shows being aired at that time. The show (I was told) was a kind of "Baby Snooks" characterization of the odd but amusing incidents in the everyday life of a "new arrival" in the metropolitan area of New York City. I believe her husband was involved as producer or director of the show, and I knew that our commercial often aired prior to the opening of the program or at its close.

At one point when Lilia was planning an episode dealing with the amusing but odd experiences surrounding Popa's efforts to communicate in her second language, English, Lilia invited me to be present in the studio audience to evaluate the accuracy of her portrayal. I was pleased to accept and was there on the evening of the performance.

The show was a humorous mixture of "Span-English" dialogue and the very descriptive facial and body expressions and gestures of an animated Popa . . . delivered to the laughter and delight of the studio audience, and I was certain, to the complete enjoyment of the at-home viewers. The show appeared to end to the applause of the studio audience after which a very curious thing happened.

Lilia motioned the audience to silence . . . and speaking directly into the camera asked Mr. Frank J. Ferraro, founder and president of the Spanish-American Institute, to please step onto the stage. I complied . . . I'm sure surprise written all over my face . . . as Lilia, stepping out of her Popa role, took my hand and as best as I can paraphrase:

"We've had lots of fun tonight," she said in her native Spanish, "but learning to speak English is necessary to a productive, successful, and happy life in the U.S.A." Then placing her hand on my shoulder . . . and in her very best English: "I learned my English at the Spanish-American Institute." The smile on her face . . . warm and friendly . . . mirrored her sincerity.

The studio audience again applauded . . . the tiny red light snapped out as the camera shut down . . . an end to one of the finest compliments we had ever received. And what a surprise . . . but not the last of the surprises. There would be another rather soon . . . another surprise to come . . . sit tight!

The most wonderful thing about life is that on most

days things go along rather smoothly . . . somewhat routinely . . . up in the morning, all is okay: breakfast . . . commute to workplace, no tie-ups . . . meaningful office work duties accomplished with the help of competent colleagues . . . satisfactory and constructive contacts with individuals visibly pleased with their day and your contributions to their efforts . . . a sensible lunch and, after an afternoon of accomplishment, the return home and the loving companionship of wife and family.

Suppertime and the quiet serenity of evening . . . entertainment . . . relaxation . . . and with nightfall, the bedrest that prepares the mind and body for a new tomorrow of achievement and the gentle passage of day-to-day that when taken together comprise a lifetime during which most things go rather smoothly . . . except for the sudden and completely unexpected SURPRISES.

A group of students coming together informally in the student lounge at the SAI

A candid photo of an ESL group enjoying "spoken English" in the SAI language laboratory

A typical group of graduates in full-dress caps and gowns celebrating the successful completion of studies at the Institute

The Institute's Puerto Rican Day float and a group of students proudly rolling down 5th Avenue

The SAI electric sign at the 43rd Street corner at Broadway in Times Square . . . recently removed to accommodate the restoration of the Paramount Theatre Marquee

A still photo of a prop used in Spanish language TV commercials depicting actual students who tell why they study at the SAI, with the author directing the commercial

A student at work in the computer class at the Institute which currently provides "hands on" training in all aspects of computer operation

7

The Institute's progress was very positive as we moved through the mid-60s in the Hotel King Edward. Our faculty and staff were a loyal and effective team . . . the student population was stable and enrollments augured well for future growth. We were steadily upgrading equipment . . . updating textbooks . . . and refining our curriculum to include Business English, Commercial Correspondence, Business Math and Machine transcription.

Suffice to say that things were going ahead rather smoothly in the fall of 1966 when I was informed that Mrs. McQuen, assistant manager of the hotel, asked that I get in touch with her at my earliest convenience, and within the hour, I stepped into her office. We exchanged the usual pleasantries after which she informed me that Miss Candia (the hotel owner) had returned to her family home . . . would not be around too much because she was seeking to sell the hotel . . . in fact, the process was already under way, though not yet finalized, and she wanted to make us aware of the pending change of ownership.

Of course this would have no bearing on the Institute . . . our lease was to 1969 . . . and while I was surprised, there seemed to be no urgency and I informed Mrs. McQuen that we were satisfied at the hotel and had every intention of continuing to the term of our lease and hopefully beyond . . . conditions permitting. She again mentioned that the sale was not yet finalized, but that if and when it was, she would introduce us to the new owner. This seemed well enough, and so the matter stood for about seven or eight weeks when we were notified that the sale had been consummated and Mrs. McQuen introduced us to the new owner.

We went together to the sixth floor where (I was told) the new owner was living, for the time being, in a suite of six rooms ... and upon entering I was introduced to a middle-aged man, somewhat short and thin in stature, rather informally dressed ... but then he was in his own home ... and a man's home is his castle!

Mrs. McQuen introduced us and to this day, I am embarrassed to admit, I can't for the life of me remember his name. It was not that he did anything bad or wrong ... it was just that he did not get involved in a person-to-person way ... and when Mrs. McQuen left the room, because she had to return to the reception desk ... he (Mr. Owner) notified me that his plan was to condominiomize the entire hotel building. He planned to sell units to people who desired a "Pied-a-Terre" (I hope I've spelled it right) ... a residence in the heart of the city where they could walk to work ... have easy access to the best shopping ... and be close at hand to the entertainment and recreational offerings of this great city without the need for automobile, subway, bus, and what-have-you means of transportation.

The owner knew that his plan would take time to implement and saw no reason for the Institute to be concerned. He would comply fully with the lease ... he had been told by Miss Candia that we were responsible tenants ... at the same time, he advised me that if at any time (prior to the expiration of the lease) we found it to our advantage to relocate, he was willing to discontinue the lease by mutual agreement without penalty to either party.

I understood his message ... responding that it was our intention to continue our tenancy ... we liked the facility but would keep in touch if the situation changed. I wished him the very best of good luck and returned to my daily responsibilities at the Institute. As I mentioned earlier, the most wonderful thing about life is that on most days things go along rather smoothly, then suddenly: surprise!

As the weeks went by, we saw no evidence of the new ownership. The staff seemed the same, Mrs. McQuen was evident in her management role . . . our contact was directly with her and we saw almost nothing of the owner. In time we did notice posters and signs on the building's marquee and in the lobby advertising the availability of condo suites, apartments and units . . . and whatever fruits these efforts bore did in no way conflict with our routine at the Institute.

In the closing weeks of 1966, Mrs. McQuen delivered a notice to our office through which the owner repeated his offer in writing: that he would honor the terms of our lease agreement, but if at any time it became advantageous for us to relocate, the hotel ownership would release the Institute from all lease obligations without penalty. The only requirement on the owner's part was that he be notified of our intention to vacate at least two months prior to any move and that all rentals be up-to-date.

We took due note of the notice and filed it carefully in the fireproof-important-document box that we kept in the lower drawer of our office file cabinet.

The decade of the 60s ushered in great changes at the Institute, not so much from the standpoint of the job we were doing, but more so in the manner in which we were viewed by the community-at-large. Our expanded use of the TV commercial carried our message directly into the homes of men and women eager to prepare, through education and training, to take advantage of opportunities available in their newfound homeland. The Institute's message resonated in the households of Spanish-speaking families and often became the topic of conversation among the elders and youth of the family . . . and closely knit as the Latino family is, oftentimes resulted in a visit to the Institute and an enrollment.

My personal experience, having appeared as the "talking head" in so many of our commercials, convinced me that our TV spots must depict real students in real classroom situations. No make-up, no fancy dress-up, no special effects . . . real people in real time making the best of their potential through education and training.

And Shalom, being the "give and take" person that he was, accepted my input after which our TV shoot required a cast of actual students filmed on the actual grounds of the Institute. Special thanks also to the photographic "genius" of Lew Merrim, who framed each shot and segment . . . working with an inexperienced cast of real students with patience and professionalism. And almost all of our commercials ended with one or another of these closing thoughts: *"Visitenos en el Spanish-American Institute, dedicada al exito de personas de habla Castellana."* (Visit us at the SAI, dedicated to the success of Spanish-speaking people.) Or *"Visitenos en el Spanish-American Institute, su futuro le espera!"* (Visit us at the SAI, your future awaits you!) Or the full face of a student on camera: *"mi nombre es* (says his/her name), *vino de* (says name of native country) and then with a smile: "I learned my English at the Spanish-American Institute."

The unexpected bonus element of these TV spots was that the students absolutely loved being "on air." They told their families and friends that they would be on television . . . the channel and time so that they would watch . . . and the sense of pride and accomplishment in what they were doing through education to prepare for a better tomorrow . . . I just knew . . . did not only congratulate the single individual's efforts, but served to encourage countless others to aspire to similar goals.

The impact of television had a tremendous effect on the

development of the Institute . . . but the impact on life in American, and in particular, life on Broadway, was absolutely volcanic . . . and would in a very few years have a very direct influence on the Institute's future.

I believe I may have had slightly more of an idea of what was happening on Broadway of the 60s . . . so much of my adult life revolved around that area . . . but in the interest of accuracy, I would like to quote from the accounts of individuals who knew first hand and in detail exactly what the condition of Broadway became with the advent of television:

"It marks the end of the road for Broadway as a midway of movie glamour. Not long ago there was glitter aplenty; air conditioned never never lands like the Roxy, the Capitol, the Rivoli, the Strand, and Loew's State were packing 'em in with first-run movies and lively stage shows. But the Roxy made way for an office building in 1960, and the others, with drastically shrunken auditoriums, are showing long-run epics on a two-a-day plan.

"The passing of the Paramount means more than the shuttering of just another movie house. It marks the end of the road for Broadway as a midway of movie glamor . . .

"The Paramount became the No. 1 haven of the bobbysoxers. There was dancing in the aisles to the swing greats such as Benny Goodman, the Dorseys, et. al. . . . Here Frank Sinatra reached the peak of his popularity . . . (but) with the coming of television, it became crystal clear to performers like Sinatra, Martin & Lewis, Bob Hope and others, that an hour before the TV camera would buy a lot more Aston-Martins, swimming pools and race horses than a week's grind at the Paramount.

"Name acts simply priced themselves out of the business. In recent years (after closing in 1964) the theater had a noisy success with rock-and-roll stage shows during holiday weeks . . . (and) patronage at the Paramount was sparse indeed.

"The brutal economics of the theater business—a mystique of grosses, percentages, union demands, film rentals, and light bulbs—all conspired to doom the Paramount, just as they had such monuments to a bygone era as the Fox in San Francisco and the Roxy in New York.

"Many Paramounts sprung up across the nation (but) . . . no other epitomized the golden age of the movie palace the way this one did. It was the paramount of Paramount."[*]

---

[*]*Publix Theatres*: Annual No. 3–1976. Published by Theatre Historical Society, pgs. 39 and 40.

8

It was well into 1967 before I undertook rather frequent daily visits to 1501 Broadway at 43rd Street. Massive renovations were under way: the gutting out of the large dome-shaped Paramount Theater and eventually the reconstruction of the second to eighth floors of the twenty-plus story office building. The need to carefully remove and preserve so very many of the theater's valuable artistic treasures understandably delayed the rebuilding and reconstruction process. While the removal of the massive theater marquee, overlooking Broadway, was quite evident when it happened, the words of John F. Barry, director of Publix Theatre Managers' Training School, makes real to the inexperienced, the massive nature of the preservation task that preceded the final renovation:

"The Paramount Theatre—with its grand lobby one hundred and sixty feet long—its foyer of imported marbles and bronze, rare paintings and beautiful tapestries—grand staircases—the great promenade circling the upper part of the theatre with a Motion Picture hall of Fame containing portraits and historical material of the more notable figures and achievements in the history of the cinema—its radio broadcasting station—its mighty stage with lifting platforms—its great organ with towering pipes . . ."

"Within the foyer of the Paramount Theatre (was) a panel in which was set a stone from every country of the world."

And so the work progressed slowly until I was finally able to enter the "work area" of the lower floors, which were finally in the rebuilding process. The project was massive

... the work crew considerable ... and as I looked, I wondered ... "Could there be a permanent home here for the Spanish-American Institute?"

I don't know how many visits I made ... just looking around ... just wondering ... and no one questioned my presence ... I think they may have supposed that somehow I belonged. I finally asked one of the workers if any of the space was available for rental. He knew nothing about that ... the office was on the seventeenth floor, and he guessed they could help me. I thanked him and within myself, I knew that in a few days or so I would stop into the building offices, which were indeed on the seventeenth floor. Two wide, thick glass doors opened from the corridor into a reception area ... four chairs against the far wall behind a small rectangular table laden with an assortment of current magazines ... and at the other end a large desk and the ever-present receptionist:

"May I help you?"

"I'd like information about renting space."

She nodded ... then motioning toward the seating area ... "Please have a seat. We'll be right with you."

I did that. She picked up the desk phone receiver ... her well-manicured slender finger quickly dialed several numbers.

"There's a gentleman for available space." She listened for a moment, then hung up. ... "In a few minutes," she said, looking across to where I sat. "Your name?" she asked.

"Frank Ferraro," I responded. "F-E-R-R-A-R-O." She made note.

A soft "buzz" on her desktop signaled that my time had come and she directed me into a very large office area divided into many individual work stations leading off of a long corridor at the extreme end of which was a large, well-furnished executive office.

We entered, and to the gentleman seated behind the desk, "Mr. Ferraro," she said, "about available space."

"Thank you, Jessie," he responded. She turned and left ... and extending his hand directly toward me, "Fred Wilpon," he said. "Please have a seat, Mr. Ferraro. What can we do for you?"

I was about forty years old, at the time ... and he seemed about the same age ... perhaps a few years younger. His demeanor was both professional and friendly, and I felt very comfortable early on in this our very first meeting. Our conversation centered around the availability of space and his interest in learning about us and the possibility of our tenancy at 1501 Broadway.

I briefly outlined the history of the Institute ... our beginning in 1955 ... previous locations ... size of student body and the fact that they were all at least seventeen years of age ... that our classes were in session all year round ... that our school day was from 9:00 A.M. to 9:00 P.M. Monday to Friday ... the make-up of our faculty and staff and a sketch of the space we now occupied at the Hotel King Edward. Mr. Wilpon, for his part, was a good listener, but he cautioned that there were still months of construction ahead before space could be ready for occupancy ... and I indicated that we were under no immediate pressure to relocate; we could wait out the construction period.

Our meeting basically ended on his note. Mr. Wilpon suggested that we get together in a couple of weeks. He thought he might have more information for us about construction progress and building management requirements. I agreed ... we exchanged a friendly handshake, after which I made my way along the long corridor to the reception area ... thanked the receptionist, and after a brief elevator "wait" descended to the lobby level and exited 1501 Broadway.

My feeling was up-beat. I thought it was a good meeting . . . but above all else that transpired, there was one brief comment early in our conversation that stuck firmly in my mind . . . a glimmer of real hope.

Early on, Mr. Wilpon asked, "What business are you in?"

"A private school of English language and commercial studies."

Mr. Wilpon: "A school . . . that's interesting . . . the building could use something like that."

And that was it. Of all the things we said, this brief exchange remained firmly set in my mind . . . a source of hope.

The next few weeks took like a year to pass, but finally a second meeting wherein Mr. Wilpon outlined several definite ideas, re: a possible Institute tenancy. The Institute would have to occupy second-floor space . . . student body traffic on the 1501 Broadway entrance and elevators was to be avoided. The Institute would be assigned the 43rd Street entrance and access by stairway to the second floor. This formerly had been the "stage door entrance" to the Paramount Theater (address 215 West 43rd Street) attached to the east end of the *New York Times* building.

Available second floor space . . . about 15,000 square feet . . . which might satisfy the needs of the Institute, and Mr. Wilpon suggested that we might tour the space, while it was still under construction, to get a "feel" for its potential. He also mentioned that another large portion of the second floor, overlooking Broadway, had already been secured by the Chemical Bank. A separate escalator entrance to the bank (from the street level) was presently under construction at the Broadway entrance to 1501.

We were certainly still interested. We would make several tours of the space in the coming weeks, and we would appreciate further details re: construction costs to us (if any) . . . terms of lease . . . required rent . . . and perhaps some insight into possible occupancy dates. This was, perhaps, the next step in our relationship . . . plans seemed to be moving ever so slowly . . . but forward, and time was on our side.

In the weeks that followed, Dave and I made several visits to the second floor area . . . and though the space was still wide open and undivided, it seemed to have the feeling of "right" for us. On other visits with Hy, our accountant, and a few very senior faculty and staff . . . all reacted positively . . . it seemed "right," and we were encouraged (as if that was necessary) to pursue the possibility.

As for myself, I was absolutely overjoyed . . . no, ecstatic is the better word, in the feeling that perhaps, finally after twenty years in the Broadway neighborhood, I would, through the Spanish-American Institute, find my permanent "career" home in Times Square!

This thing with me about Broadway and Times Square goes way back to my childhood when I lived very close to my grandparents and for about five of my pre-teen years lived in their household. They spoke Italian . . . knew no English . . . in fact my grandfather, never having attended school, referred to himself (in Italian) as a man "without alphabet." But could he tell stories about his hometown and its people in Italy! And could he recite proverbs and old sayings relative to all aspects of living and dying.

We were very close, my grandpa and I, and because I heard his stories, proverbs, and old sayings so very often, I became proficient in repeating them in the Italian I learned very early in life. In fact it was not uncommon for Grandpa (in the company of his friends who were frequent visitors) to ask me to repeat that story, proverb or saying for the benefit of his company of friends. I readily and happily complied . . . sometimes to the surprise of my audience, but ALWAYS to the absolute enjoyment of my grandpa . . . his face lighting up in a complete expression of joy . . . his chest bursting with pride . . .

"This one will make a million on Broadway!" He said it so many times on different occasions following my recitations that it remained in my subconsciousness for all the days of my life. And then in 1945 as a corporal in the U.S. Army, having returned from the ETO on a ten-day furlough before shipping out (rumor had it) for service in the Pacific against Japan . . . where was I on V-J Day? Celebrating V-E Day in TIMES SQUARE!!

And what a time it was. Before my furlough ended, Japan surrendered and all talk of further overseas duty evaporated. I completed my tour of duty at Fort Bragg, North Carolina, with an honorable discharge in 1946. After that my immediate goal: college enrollment, and as an undergraduate, I became Feature Editor of the campus newspaper at Bergen Junior College in Teaneck, New Jersey, and later at Adelphi University in Garden City, New York. As feature editor I enjoyed the luxury of selecting my own subjects . . . and yes, I chose Broadway as my beat.

One of my first articles was an interview with Pamela Brown, a British actress, appearing at the Royal Theater on Broadway in *The Importance of Being Earnest*. She had also had a notable role in the movie, *One of Our Aircraft Is Missing*.

Another interview was with Beryl Davis, a vocalist, appearing at the Strand Theater and a regular each Wednesday evening on the Phil Silvers' Radio program. Then Lisa Kirk at the Century Theater in *Kiss Me Kate*, and Judith Anderson in *Medea* at the National Theater on Broadway. There was an interview with June Lockhart in *For Love or Money* at the Henry Miller Theater . . . and Stan Kenton at the Paramount theater in September of 1947 and a bit later with June Christy, lead female vocalist in the Kenton band . . . and another visit to the Paramount theater to interview Vic Damone.

Each of these experiences was special for me, but the absolutely most unforgettable was my interview with James Stewart when he starred in *Harvey* at the 48th Street Theater. But let me begin at the beginning.

In the hope of gaining an interview with James Stewart, I made my way along the narrow alley passageway that led to the stage door entrance to the theater. I entered and about three or four steps inside was met by a security guard.

"Need anything?" he asked.

"I'd like to interview Mr. Stewart for my college newspaper."

"Mr. Stewart is not here," he responded rather brusquely. "And he's not doing interviews. He's too busy."

I don't know that I said anything . . . simply exited the stage door and walked along the alleyway . . . returning to the sidewalk at 48th Street . . . and miracle of miracles at that moment, a yellow cab drove up along curbside, stopped . . . the rear door opened and out stepped James Stewart exactly in my direction.

"Mr. Stewart," I managed. "I'd appreciate an interview with you for my college paper."

I was barely 5 feet 5 1/2 inches tall . . . James Stewart was the Empire State Building by comparison . . . but in one graceful motion, he placed his arm about my shoulder . . . "You bet we can," he said, and together we walked briskly along the alleyway . . . entered the stage door . . . walked by the security guard who looked past me as he nodded "hello" to Mr. Stewart. We made our way to the dressing room and the interview, which has always been one of my most cherished memories of a gentleman who was, without a doubt, the very best among God's finest.

And when I found my first teaching job . . . where

would it be but on 42nd Street three quarters of the way up from Broadway, just below Sixth Avenue. Is it any wonder that the prospect of a permanent home for the Institute on 43rd Street and Broadway, in the very heart of Times Square, if it came to pass would be, for me, a dream come true!

At long last we received a written proposal from the 1499-1501 Broadway Company, presenting the basics of a lease agreement. Construction was still under way, but going forward; decisions would have to be made to meet tenant specific needs. Acceptance of the lease proposals would signify a "green light" for the area to be divided by the landlord's architect and space designers in close contact with the tenant's representatives. The proposal specified the rental of the second floor (approximately fifteen thousand square feet) to be used by the Spanish-American Institute for "classrooms, lounge, administrative offices, and bookstore for the exclusive use of teachers and pupils of tenant's school." Term of the lease was set at ten years at the rental rate of $89,602.50 per annum. Attached to the proposal was exhibit "A" . . . a plan of the second floor space without interior partitions, which indicated that the Institute's space would run from the 43rd Street side of the building clear through to the 44th Street side.

Our reactions to the proposal were immediate and favorable . . . and we signed on the proverbial "dotted line," patiently awaiting the next step, which was not all far behind. On April 8, 1968, the Institute (as tenant) signed a ten-year lease with the 1499-1501 Broadway Company (as landlord), which provisions were as outlined in the earlier proposal . . . the term being as follows: To begin July 1, 1968 and continuing for ten years to June 30, 1978.

There were provisions re: utility charges, tenant/landlord upkeep responsibilities, the need to adhere to local, state, and federal laws, et. al., but none of these "tiny print" stipulations raised any "red flags" and the lease was executed: signed and sealed. We lost no time advising management at the King Edward Hotel of our plan to vacate by July 1, 1968 . . . and in accordance with previous agreements, our notice to vacate was accepted in stride by all concerned.

The weeks between April 8th and July 1, 1968 were replete with meetings with the architect and space designer individuals charged with the final development of our second floor area. They helped us mightily to realize the most efficient use of our space, and we were truly blessed to have their "know-how" at our disposal. And, lest you think the daily classroom activity and student-teacher learning processes took a back seat to location . . . location . . . location, let me assure you that our scholastic activity was upheld throughout. We gradually informed and notified all interested parties of our impending relocation plans . . . and to our knowledge, the future was being anticipated with good feelings and a sense of excitement by all concerned.

9

On July 1, 1968, the Institute, with the help of a professional moving company, moved lot, stock, and barrel into 215 West 43rd Street . . . the former Paramount Theater stage door entrance, which thereafter came to be known as the entrance to the Spanish-American Institute!

Reaction to the new facility exceeded all expectations: everything was so new . . . the lighting so bright and adequate . . . the air conditioning so effective . . . and a walk from the "machine room" with its four large windows overlooking Shubert Alley on 44th Street, through the wide hallways past the spacious classrooms on the 43rd Street end of the second floor, with its three large windows overlooking the busy street below, all contributed to our good feelings of satisfaction with the Institute's "new home."

And on each window in gold lettering for all the world to see: Spanish-American Institute, School of Business, English, and IBM. A "plus" was the fact that our 43rd Street side abutted the east end of the *New York Times* building . . . a benefit because the area was so well-lighted during evening and nighttime hours, and there was almost one security guard on duty at all times in addition to the constant flow of pedestrians during all hours of the day. These conditions gave our students an added sense of security during a period when many families worried about the safety of New York City streets.

And so it was that we settled comfortably into our new home. The facility was essentially provided by the landlord . . . our responsibility was limited to requirements specifically desired by the operation of our school. We installed an automatic bell system to sound the beginning and end of class times, and an intercom system connecting the office to classrooms in addition to multi-station telephones. Of course there were the moving expenses and the purchase of additional furniture to fit our new situation . . . but all in all, we managed our finances without the need for loans or outside financing . . . an accomplishment we had achieved over all our years since 1955.

And then there was the CANOPY . . . but let me explain:

It seems that our landlord had entered into negotiations with an organization seeking space on the eighth floor . . . and because the proposed tenant was engaged in a business that might infringe upon the lease agreement between the Institute and the landlord, we were asked if we would consent to revision in our lease, which would protect our situation at the same time make it possible for the landlord to lease the eighth floor area to the "new" tenant.

In a nutshell, it came down to this . . . we at this Institute were teaching the operation of IBM equipment . . . the incoming 8th floor tenant was in the business of advising companies on the installation, repair, and operation of IBM machinery. They were deeply involved in the technology and in no way in the teaching as was the case at the Institute.

We considered the proposition and saw no reason to be negative; the landlord had been very fair and up front in his dealings with us . . . and his desire was to achieve this 8th floor tenancy . . . and he suggested that we might be in some way compensated for our cooperation . . . SOOO . . .

There was really one thing we would like to have at the 215 West 43rd Street entrance to the Institute . . . A CANOPY!!!

And so it was, no sooner said than done, on the second day of December 1968, new leases were drawn up . . . revised . . . amended and signed to the satisfaction of all concerned . . . including the landlord's agreement to provide a canopy at the Institute's 43rd Street entrance. And this canopy, from building to curbside, afforded easy visibility to passers-by along Broadway looking west toward 8th Avenue and those walking east along 43rd Street toward Times Square. As I indicated, the situation was resolved to everyone's satisfaction . . . and we couldn't be happier.

As in the past, course offerings were revised and expanded to keep up with rapidly changing technology. Courses in Comptometry, IBM Keypunch, and Computer Programming RPG on the 360/20 console were added to our secretarial and business programs . . . and an English language lab was introduced and utilized to increase the student's exposure to conversational English. Our facility had grown to include twenty-two classrooms, including our "machine room" with about fifty Royal manual and IBM Selectric typewriters, the student lounge, bookstore, reception area, and the Institute offices . . . divided into six rather private interview and/or student guidance stations. Our faculty and staff grew in accordance with Institute needs. My son, Dante Ferraro, in his senior college year, came aboard in 1969 to lend his hands to our efforts, and continued to serve in various capacities upon his graduation from Fordham University.

A few years later in 1971, my son-in-law, Robert Connelly, then in his senior year, came aboard to assist in our efforts and remained with the Institute upon his graduation from Fairleigh Dickenson University. Finally, just ten years later in 1982, Paul Schiffman, Dave's son, came aboard upon his graduation from Hofstra University. Our faculty and staff were so very important to the daily life, growth and evolution of the Institute . . . their efforts merit the most honorable and frequent mention in any history of the Institute's development and progress. And the last three named:

Dante, Robert, Paul . . . they came for the duration and then some . . . STAY TUNED!!!

Notification came directly from the New York State Department of Education in Albany requiring that, henceforth, private schools and institutes would have to qualify for registration with their department in order to continue to provide educational services in the State of New York. A procedure and time frame were provided whereby an institution, in compliance with State Education guidelines, would be properly registered and able to continue its educational services. We were eager to participate and hopefully, at the earliest, gain the newly required State Education Department registration.

I could not help at this time, several months into 1970, recalling the advice received about fifteen years earlier from a wise gentleman . . . an official in the Education Department, Washington, D.C., who had taken the time to visit the Institute and upon taking his leave left me with these words of advice: "You have a very good thing going here," he said. "Keep doing what you are doing . . . develop it . . . expand it to the very best of your ability . . . and don't worry about approvals, government agencies, and certifications . . . if you develop seriously and well, these agencies will eventually seek you out and recognize your efforts."

It had finally come to pass, and we lost little time in our desire and efforts to make State Department of Education registration a reality . . . but it did take time.

There were several visits to Albany during which Dave and I met with Education Department supervisors and staff. We received orientation and outlines of the requirements expected of the Institute as we moved through the process. These meetings were very constructive, and the helpful assistance extended by the department staff were a source of encouragement. In time we were advised that a Mr.

Obermeyer was assigned as our department contact, and the process continued.

We were required to outline the history of the Institute ... the educational background of its founders ... the make-up and qualifications of faculty and staff ... a complete description of courses offered ... required class hours ... examination schedules and grading criteria, in addition to textbook usage ... attendance requirements and record keeping ... tuition costs and payment plans. At the same time, Institute financial and accounting records were requested by and made available to the State Department of Education. There was an evaluation of the Institute's facility regarding number and size of classrooms ... student furniture: tablet armchairs ... desks ... blackboards ... faculty and student storage facilities ... type, model and number of typewriters, IBM equipment, comptometers, and the use of language laboratory equipment. An evaluation of toilet facilities ... the adequacy of classroom lighting ... the availability of sprinkler and fire alarm systems in addition to an evaluation of the means of emergency egress ... the frequency of fire drills and the designation of "fire marshalls" among the faculty and staff able to act effectively in the event of need.

The Institute was required to submit actual copies of ads: newspaper, magazine, and actual copies of radio and TV commercials and the stations used. The department was interested in the nature of claims made and/or whether unrealistic guarantees or promises of success (as the guarantee of immediate high-paying office employment) or "learn two years of English in two months" ... false claims, to say the least, bandied about in some quarters, but which were never a part of our message to our students or the community-at-large. At one point in our contact with the State Education Department, a portion of their staff were assigned to offices in the Twin Towers ... their workload in NYC so heavy (I was told) that it was economical, time-wise, to station some staff locally to enhance their availability and effectiveness. This change made Mr. Obermeyer and others more easily accessible to us, which together with their helpfulness and cooperation, advanced our march toward eventual registration.

Another aspect of the process included "one-on-one" interviews that Mr. Obermeyer and his aides held with Institute faculty, staff, and students ... in addition to class visitations to evaluate student-teacher interaction in the classroom setting and subject matter presentation.

I was very pleased when (on several occasions following these interviews and/or class visitations) the evaluator expressed to me how impressed he was with the high regard to which teachers and students held each other and their very positive attitude toward the Institute.

And so it was we made our way through the process. Was everything just perfect? Of course not ... but very much of what we were doing was on the right track ... and with modest revisions and safeguards, the Institute's policies and programs would meet registration requirements.

For example a very clear "non-discrimination policy" statement was required in the school catalogue ... tuition refund policy was to be clearly defined and accurate statistics re: student "drop-out rates," in addition to employment placement data were to be accurately recorded for evaluation. The Institute had thus far granted certificates to indicate successful course completions, and (after Institute registration) diplomas would be granted to students completing credit-hours in designated programs of study.

These were among the "hurdles" that had to be overcome on the road to registration: our constant attention, and the unselfish assistance and guidance of Mr. Obermeyer and

Department of Education staff finally achieved the desired goal:

The Spanish-American Institute was accepted as a Registered Private Business School by the New York State Department of Education in 1973!!!!

I must take pause right here and now to make you aware of our IBM episode . . . no real problem, to be sure, simply a tale about what may (at times) befall "a pebble" caught in the whirlpool of CORPORATE GROWTH vs. GOVERNMENT CONTROL!! . . . Oh, my goodness.

A vital part of the efficient operation of an organization and certainly of an educational institution is to keep its faculty and students abreast of changing methods and technologies to equip their students with "real time" abilities in the business world. The increasingly rapid changing technologies of the 1960s and 70s presented all serious organizations . . . educational or otherwise . . . with the necessity of "keeping up or dropping out."

The Institute systematically went from manual to electric typewriters and knew the excitement of the IBM Selectric typewriter . . . its spinning round ball replacing the sliding carriage . . . and later the bookkeeping machine and the transcription equipment with its cassette tape . . . expected to replace the need for secretaries to master stenography systems.

The executive simply dictated his letters, memos, et. al., on to a cassette tape at his leisure (in or away from his office) . . . placed the tape into the appropriate box from which the transcriber (donning the proper headphones) transcribed the material without the necessary presence of the executive. This system gradually led to the creation of the "steno pool" ... a group of transcribers under the watchful eye of the transcription department supervisor, who made efforts to assure that copy was produced free of spelling, grammatical, and what-have-you typing errors.

These were among the technological advances that moved us into the world of IBM keypunch machines ... keypunch cards ... the sorter and the IBM Computer 360/20 R.P.G. The introduction of these IBM systems into the world of everyday business demanded that prospective employees (our students) be adequately prepared to meet these needs. And so it was that the Institute expanded curriculum to include as much IBM technology as we could afford ... including not only the acquisition of competent faculty and the allocation of suitable space, but the financial cost of rentals payable to the IBM Corporation.

Our relationship with this giant of companies was never anything but the very best. Their field reps assisted in the development of our "instructional procedures," and qualified IBM staff were readily available when we required their expert assistance. Our faculty were frequently invited to IBM uptown Manhattan headquarters for instructional seminars ... and in all our dealings with every level of IBM personnel, at the Institute or in their offices, I never ceased to be impressed with their competence, careful attention to our needs, and the respect in which they regarded our efforts ... small as they were in comparison to the vastness of IBM.

And so it was about the mid-1970s that the IBM rep stepped into the Institute office ... asked how things were going and wondered if we would be interested in OWNING the IBM equipment we were now and had been previously leasing.

Of course we would, but ...

He then pointed out that the Institute could purchase for the sum of ONE DOLLAR the machinery we were now renting . . . and the purchase would include a service agreement. I thought he was kidding . . . but he wasn't, and in a very short time, the documentation was completed and the "deal" consummated. When I later wondered Why? . . . I was told that the Institute was being presented as an example of a small independent company's ability to OWN (rather than restricted to leasing) IBM equipment. Years later when I checked into the accuracy of this claim: U.S. v IBM Antitrust, I found no specific reference to the Spanish-American Institute . . . but I did find this District Court ruling: "applicable to IBM . . . (that) IBM is hereby ordered and directed, beginning not later than one year after the entry of this Final Judgment, to offer to sell at any time . . . to the lessee of any IBM tabulating or electronic data processing each such machine being used by such lessee" . . . [*]

And so ends the tale of our IBM episode . . . or better still, an insight into what can at times befall a "pebble" caught in the whirlpool of CORPORATE GROWTH vs. GOVERNMENT CONTROL!! Oh, my goodness.

---

[*]U.S. District Court: for the Southern District of N.Y. United States of America, Plaintiff, v. International Business Machines Corporations, Defendant. Civil Action No. 72_344.

10

The New York State Department of Education registration was a giant step forward for the Institute, which also, since 1955, authorizes under federal law to enroll non-immigrant alien students. Approvals that led to participation in student loan programs and opened the way to expanded curriculums, such as, GED (high school equivalency diploma preparation) and TOEFL (teaching of English as a foreign language) Exam preparation . . . and in a bit of a role reversal, several local colleges were recommending that their incoming (fall semester students) pursue summer session ESL classes at the Institute to better cope with college-level textbooks. The fact that a summer session course at SAI was considerably more reasonable than the tuition cost in most colleges, I suspect, also played in the Institute's favor . . . and we were thankful for that.

In the mid-70s our student body was made up of men and women of almost every nation in South and Central America, Jamaica, Haiti, Cuba, Puerto Rico, Dominican Republic, Spain, Italy, the Middle East, Japan, China, Formosa, Turkey, Laos, Poland, Iran, the Philippines, Yugoslavia, Korea, and the United States. Our student body was growing in this period of inflation and extreme gasoline and fuel oil shortages . . . and what we read and heard was that periods of economic stress and unemployment almost always led to increased school enrollments . . . in difficult times more people seek through re-education and training to better equip themselves for success in the changing economic climate.

Another interesting trend, we noticed, was that a growing number of our students were planning to enroll in colleges and universities after completion of their SAI courses.

In the past we were most often asked to verify a student's qualifications for office positions: secretary, receptionist, typist, bookkeeping assistant, import-export clerk, etc. We were now more and more being asked to submit a transcript to THUS and SO college or university . . . on behalf of one of our graduates seeking admission to the education department in preparation for a teaching career . . . or the engineering department of a college to broaden and expand upon education begun in their native land . . . but for one reason or another interrupted . . . but now could be resumed (hopefully in part to the positive influence of the Institute).

It was amazing to become aware of the very intelligent, well-trained, able and ambitious men and women who were forced to abandon (often for political reasons) not only their family and home but those dreams of which futures are made. I know that my awareness of these situations and the role that the Institute played in the realization of so many dreams in the lives of so many good people was a source of constant personal satisfaction . . . in addition to the feeling of pride and love that I felt for my country . . . that it could do so very much for so very many . . . including me!

One afternoon the receptionist buzzed my intercom phone: "Mr. Ferraro, there's a gentleman from *The New York Times* to see you."

I entered the reception area and invited an elderly, well-dressed, rather tall gentleman to "please come in" . . . whereupon we both took the ten or twelves steps into my office and he said: "Mr. Ferraro, I'm Mr. Sulzberger's private secretary . . . and he's asked me to speak with you about your canopy . . . at the 43rd Street school entrance. He's very upset about the canopy . . ."

I won't attempt to further quote the secretary's exact words, but the message was that Mr. Sulzberger was very upset about the canopy because it detracted from the *The*

New York Times image running west from Broadway to Eighth Avenue. I assured the secretary that it was never our intention to accomplish anything more than properly making visible to the general public the entrance to the Institute. He did not dispute that and suggested that if we removed the canopy, the design (or art) department of the *Times*, at no expense to the Institute, would design and install an acceptable replacement that would be (more against the building) but still clearly indicate the Institute's entrance.

It seemed like a very generous offer . . . gently made . . . but I wasn't completely "sold" on the idea. I felt it was important for the Institute to maintain its (street side) visibility . . . whereupon the secretary repeated that the changes would be provided at no cost to the Institute . . . and suddenly . . . BAM!!! . . . it hit me hard and clear.

I advised the secretary that although the proposal was not completely set in my mind, it might possibly come to pass if *The New York Times* provided a full-page article in its pages about the Spanish-American Institute: its history, educational mission, faculty, student body, and so forth . . . at the discretion of the reporter and editor assigned by the newspaper. We would, of course, make ourselves and the Institute completely at the disposal of the *Times* in whatever manner they required to achieve an interesting and accurate article.

An agreement along these lines, I thought, might very well satisfy all concerned . . . and the secretary, taking note of my suggestion, said he would relay the information to Mr. Sulzberger and "get back to me as soon as possible." And so it was we parted . . . and the subject never came up again . . . and the canopy continues to this day to mark the 43rd Street entrance to the SAI.

There is an aspect of this "canopy story" that bears telling. I had been through most of my adult life an avid newspaper reader: the *Daily News*, the *Mirror*, the *Herald Tribune*, the *Brooklyn Eagle*, the *Journal American* and the *New York Times* . . . and by far the publication of highest respect in my mind was *The New York Times*. It was in its pages that the complete and wholly accurate accounts of world and national events were presented daily by a staff of dedicated and qualified editors and reporters. Everything in my mind about *The New York Times* was "A-One" . . . and when there was no further action regarding my suggestion, my respect and admiration for that publication increased because I had always believed that it was impossible for anyone to "buy their way" onto those pages. My brief experience had borne out that belief . . . although it took about five years for me to fully appreciate the "fair play, good neighbor policy" of the world's premier publication. And here's the way it happened without fanfare, no strings attached:

In late August of 1980, a *New York Times* reporter, Frank Emblen, came into the Institute office indicating his desire to write an article about the work of the Institute. He wondered if he might speak with some students and faculty, inspect our facility, and use one of the *Times* photographers for any photos that might be taken to accompany the article. We promptly consented to his request and on Sunday, September 7, 1980, the article appeared in *The New York Times* under the by-line of Frank Emblen and a photo by Sara Krulwich of (a student) Ruth Lopez, taking typing at the Spanish-American Institute as her daughter, Sandra, did homework while waiting for her mom to finish class. The article's title: "AN INSTITUTE for LATINS in MANHATTAN."

(Note: the complete article appears in the Appendix.)

11

And thus we were "covered" by the respected *New York Times*. It was so very wonderful that it happened ... the more-so because it came about unsolicited ... without a price ... and appeared in one of the nation's most highly respected newspapers in my mind ... then ... is it now?

There were so many good things happening at the Institute apart from classroom activity: student field trips under faculty and staff supervision to the Public Library, museums and art exhibits, Circle Line day rips to the Statue of Liberty and combination boat ride-picnic excursions to Bear Mountain and swimming (in season) at the Anthony Wayne Pool at Harriman, New York. There was even one trip by a large group to Disney World in Orlando. Students were encouraged to invite family and friends ... many participated, and this served as an introduction to the SAI and the people who made it "tick."

The Institute's graduation exercises were among the most rewarding events to our students, their families and friends. These exercises were held semi-annually in the early years (courses were shorter) and annually, later on, when study programs from one year to eighteen months and beyond led to the formal graduation exercise: the wearing of cap and gown ... the march into the large ballroom to the inspiring notes of "Pomp and Circumstance" in the presence of several hundred friends and family ... the uplifting congratulatory speeches by invited guests ... and finally, the pride in accomplishment deeply felt by each graduate as he/she approached the podium to receive their certificate or diploma, indicating the successful completion of SAI studies.

Graduation exercises were almost always held in the main ballrooms of midtown hotels: the Hotel Diplomat was, for many years, a favorite, and the Hotel Empire, around 60th Street near Central Park . . . the Hotel Milford Plaza, and on one occasion, the Americana, on Broadway, around 50th Street. The exercises were always followed by the presentation of Miss Spanish-American Institute (selected by student body vote) and her Court of Attendants . . . usually representing a variety of eight foreign countries, sometimes including the U.S.A.

The activity was most pleasing to all involved . . . the constant clicking of cameras and the flashing of lightbulbs told us as much, in addition to the coverage that followed in *El Diario, La Prensa,* and several Spanish language magazines. For many of our students, graduation was "a dream come true" . . . an opportunity to shine . . . to be in the spotlight . . . to be recognized for their efforts and to inspire them to greater success in their "new found" homeland either through more productive employment or further education in pursuit of professional careers. For our part at the Institute, these exercises were a further validation . . . as if such was needed . . . of the effectiveness and value of our educational mission. We were kept quite busy in "daily schoolwork" activity . . . but when we paused at moments like these; we were proud.

Whatever else was happening, time was passing and our original lease at 215 West 43rd Street . . . our ten-year lease, signed in 1968, was just short of eighteen months to June 30, 1978, of completion. We were happy with our tenancy . . . our relations with the Paramount Building management was, to our knowledge, just fine . . . we had never fallen behind in the payment of our $8,000 monthly rental and utility responsibilities. There was no reason not to be able to continue our tenancy . . . BUT we thought it the better part of valor to AS SOON AS POSSIBLE enter discussions re: the renewal of our lease beyond 1978.

And so it was that on September 28, 1977, an amendment to our original lease extended our tenancy five years to June 30, 1983, at a new rental of $8,333.33 monthly, plus utility and custodial costs were agreed to and signed by all concerned . . . but there was for us, at SAI, a new and important element added . . . NOW HOLD YOUR HAT:

The Institute was granted the right to install and maintain a "store front sign" on the west 43rd Street and Broadway corner of the Paramount Building at 1501 Broadway!! Required permits would have to comply with city codes and a fully licensed sign company charged with the installation and upkeep at SAI expense. These conditions were promptly met, and a short time later, there it was for all the world to see . . . on the corner of West 43rd Street and Broadway . . . in the heart of Times Square:

Spanish-American Institute
School of
Business and English

A bit more about the sign later . . . but for now suffice to say that beyond this lease amendment, which carried the SAI to June 30, 1983, there were future agreements, which in total continued the Institute's occupancy through the 1990s and well into the 21st century. Our dealings with the several management companies from Mr. Wilpon at the outset, to Mr. Jeff Gural of Newmark & Company, throughout the 80s and to date were always conducted on a fair and mutually beneficial basis. There were several instances over the years when accommodations were requested by the landlord or tenant . . . and happily, in all cases, adjustments were made to cope with changing conditions. Cooperation was always the "password" on both ends . . . and for that we have been grateful.

There is one personal regret, if I may: I have for all my life been an avid follower and participant in the game of baseball. I played it in the playgrounds . . . the neighborhood empty lots in Brooklyn . . . on the "righties team" at the World's Fair of 1939 where we caught "fungos" off the bat of Babe Ruth (p.s. I never caught one) . . . and as a member of the "Knothole Gang" went frequently to Ebbetts Field, especially when the Giants were in town . . . my idol was Mel Ot . . . but I digress . . .

Back to my one regret: had I known in 1968, when I first met Mr. Fred Wilpon, that he would become co-owner (with Nelson Doubleday) of the New York Mets in the 1980s, and ultimately full owner in 2002, I would have been more than happy to avail Mr. Wilpon of my more than sixty-five years experience with the national pastime. I might have even considered becoming a loyal Met fan . . . but as things stand . . . oh, well . . . so be it and GOOD LUCK, Mr. Wilpon. And thank you for the kindness and understanding you extended to my dreams for the Spanish-American Institute in 1968. You were the best!!

And the Institute sign in the heart of Times Square: what a "kick" it was to me personally. I don't know how much it contributed to enrollments . . . though I was certain it had a positive effect . . . but more than that was the realization that more than a handful of people, among the thousands who passed through the area daily, would look up, see the sign: Spanish-American Institute . . . School of Business and English . . . and feel the pride: . . . "Hey, that's my school. I went there five years ago" . . . or "I know that school. My brother (sister, mother, uncle, aunt, cousin or friend) graduated from there before going to college." I knew the presence of the sign must have had this effect, and one more thing . . . on more than a few occasions, a famous celebrity performer or an entire Broadway theater cast presented "outdoor shows" on a stage built upon the triangle that runs from about 46th Street to 43rd Street and Broadway. These productions were performed to the delight of thousands of people in the area, at no charge. They were usually televised and carried on the networks as news, if not otherwise presented in their entirety.

And the greatest "kick" for me was . . . when at home and watching the TV, the screen was suddenly full of that Broadway stage: the wonderful sound of theater music . . . the magical cast of dancers . . . the inspiring lyrics of the season's greatest hits . . . and then in that moment when the TV cameraman hit a certain angle (like from the east side of 45th Street to the west side corner of 43rd Street) . . . THERE IT WAS . . . at first the Chemical (later Chase) bank sign, and in the next moment: Spanish-American Institute . . . School of Business and English.

"THERE IT IS, Angie . . . did you see it?"

"Yes, Frank, I see it. Yes, Frank, I saw it."

I don't know how many times this happened over the years until the sign was removed in 1996 as part of the Times Square Business Improvement District renovation project . . . and made room for the reconstruction of the original Paramount Theater marquee on West 43rd Street and Broadway. It was my greatest "kick" . . . seeing that sign on TV . . . and well, it was a really good feeling that I really never got over, no matter how often it happened.

By 1990, Dante Ferraro had been an active full-time member of the Institute's faculty and administration for twenty years, and held the position of Executive Director and Financial Aid Director. At the same time Robert Connelly had been an active full-time member of the faculty and administration for eighteen years, and held the position of Director of Students . . . while Paul Schiffman, the youngest of the trio, had been an active full-time member of the faculty and administration for just under ten years, and held the position of Director of Admissions and TAP Certifying Officer. The trio represented almost forty-eight years of service to the SAI and its educational mission.

The Institute has continued to retain the New York State Department of Education registration, originally bestowed in 1973, but subject to reevaluation and renewal every three to five years. The Institute continued as it had since 1955 to be authorized under federal law to enroll non-immigrant alien students with F-1 visas, form I-20. The Institute was approved since 1986, by the Accrediting Council for Independent Colleges and Schools (ACICS). Our faculty and staff have from the very beginning been a constant source of pride for their dedication to their students and the SAI. Many have served in their positions for five years and several others for ten years or more and deserve the highest of praise for their efforts.

During the 80s and well into the 90s the prevalence of the COMPUTER in every aspect of life in the world of business, played heavily upon the Institute's responsibility to equip its students to fulfill the demands of the twentieth century and beyond . . . and so it was that the curriculum expanded to offer:

IBM Computer Graphics and Keyboarding
Database Management
Introduction to DOS
Using Lotus 1-2-3
Introduction to Microsoft Windows
Introduction to Microsoft Works

I wish I were able to tell you in greater detail about each

of these areas of computer literacy . . . but being a product of the educational system of the 1940s and 50s, I can only thank the good Lord for providing the faculty who so well train and instruct our students in the efficient use and application of these computer systems in today's modern business world.

The impact of computer technology is apparent in all aspects of life . . . and by the early 1990s the Institute's "machine room" contained a hundred computers for student instruction, in addition to a computer on the desktop of each director and administrative assistant.

The SAI was administered by Dante Ferraro, Robert Connelly, and Paul Schiffman through the late 80s . . . although its co-founders, Frank Ferraro and David Schiffman, retained oversight in their capacity as president/treasurer and vice-president/secretary respectively.

In 1994 David Schiffman retired from active participation, and about eighteen months later, July 4, 1996, Frank Ferraro retired from active participation in the daily administration of the SAI.

The ownership was assumed by Dante Ferraro, Robert Connelly, and Paul Schiffman, and in 1995 ownership of the Institute was turned over to The Institute Foundation, Inc., a not-for-profit New York corporation. Its officers were established as Dante V. Ferraro, President/Treasurer . . . Paul Schiffman, Vice-President . . . and Robert Connelly, Secretary.

As I close this retrospective in the month of August 2003, I know that the Institute continues its mission under the competent management of the three able and dedicated individuals who by the year 2000 had collectively contributed more than fifty years of experience to the advancement of the Institute and its students. It was indeed a milestone when we entered the twenty-first century . . . a period of great hope for the SAI . . . and even now, after 9/11/01, the torch continues to furnish the light of education and hope in the hearts of men and women of good will.

To the Spanish-American Institute: its administrators, faculty, students past and present . . . and to all who have in some way extended a helping hand over these many years: THANK YOU and GOD BLESS!!

Epilogue

The Times Square area has undergone massive changes since the year 2000 . . . old, run-down buildings replaced by impressive office towers, modern hotels, and inviting new restaurants. Theaters have been refurbished to satisfy the ever-growing crowds of tourists and native residents out for an evening of live and cinematic entertainment. And everywhere along Broadway, the specialty shopping areas and small stores present their wares in a modern, clean, and up-beat setting.

So too have the SAI and 1501 Broadway undergone recent changes: Chemical Bank, which gave way to Chase, has left the Paramount Building for modern, new quarters at the corner of 42nd Street and Broadway. *The New York Times* has left its building on 43rd Street (except for office staff) in favor of more modern production facilities along I-95 in New Jersey.

The Institute remains at 215 West 43rd Street, where it has been since 1968, although massive renovations in the past two years have completely modernized and updated its facility to twenty-first century standards.

The Institute carries on in its educational mission under the able guidance of Dante, Paul, and Robert. The future is and has been in their hands . . . and it remains for the three of them . . . together or singly, to create and record what still lies ahead in the life of the SAI and its educational mission in the twenty-first century.

Appendix

Reprinted below is the complete article as it appeared in *The New York Times,* September 7, 1980, under the by-line of Frank Emblen:

An Institute for Latins in Manhattan

Twenty-five years ago two teachers with a dream and $500 found three students and started a school—the Spanish-American Institute. Today that school, a few steps from Times Square, opens the door of the English-speaking world to nearly three-thousand people a year, many of them native Americans.

"We were totally ignorant of the business world or we would never have done it," said David Schiffman, associate director of the institute, who came up with his $250 by borrowing on his GI insurance. "That's right," said his partner, Frank J. Ferraro, director of the institute. "Today we would know enough not to try it."

The institute, which teaches business courses as well as English as a second language, now occupies 15,000 square feet on the second floor of the Paramount Building, 215 West 43rd Street. And Mr. Ferraro and Mr. Schiffman no longer teach. They have 22 full-time and 26 part-time instructors, and the school has 30,000 alumni.

"There's nothing like doing the right thing at the right time," said Mr. Ferraro as he sat at his desk recently in a spacious office at the institute. "Teaching English to the Spanish-speaking was a whole new field then. People were there and nobody was servicing them."

Mr. Ferraro and Mr. Schiffman, both now fifty-five

years old, were in the same graduating class at New Utrecht High School in Brooklyn. After military service in World War II, they became reacquainted as graduate students at New York University, where both earned master's degrees in English. Then both became instructors at Fairleigh Dickerson University.

When they started the institute in 1955, their three students paid tuition of $10 each a week.

From three classrooms and the three students, the school has grown to 23 classrooms and more than 850 students on any school day, which starts at 9:15 A.M. and ends at 9:14 P.M.

Part of the school's appeal is the intimacy of small classes, its students say. "I knew a girl who went to another school," said Mercedes Russo, part of a class of seven in Spanish stenography.

"She didn't like it because she wasn't learning there, so she came here with me." Miss Russo, who emigrated from the Dominican Republic seven months ago, wants to be a bilingual secretary.

Most of the students are Hispanic and Mr. Ferraro, who is of Italian descent, and Mr. Schiffman, who is Jewish, spoke with affection about the cultural traits and traditions of their students.

But some Latin-American traditions cause problems.

"When a student goes for a job interview, she just can't take her mother, aunt, and cousin with her," Mr. Ferraro said. "I have to explain that an employer here just wouldn't understand."

The youngest students at the school are seventeen and on occasion a mother will insist on accompanying a daughter to and from school.

"A mother asked if she could wait for her daughter in

the student lounge," Mr. Ferraro recalled. The mother held court there for six months.

Just as some daughters who are students come with their mothers, so some mothers who are students bring along their daughters. Right now at least four mothers bring children, ages six to eight, to typing class, Mr. Ferraro said.

The institute's oldest student is Francisco Cabrera, ninety two. His file shows that he was born in Havana on January 29, 1888. It also shows that he has been absent only twice in five months and that he is not only studying English but also taking the course for the high-school equivalency examination.

"He says he wants to learn English so he can enjoy movies and TV," Mr. Ferraro said. "He wants to live all of life, not just half."

Spanish is the native language of 75 percent of the institute's students, and four out of five of these Spanish speakers are foreign born. The rest are Puerto Ricans.

Of the 25 percent of the student body that is not Spanish-speaking, Japanese make up the largest segment, followed by Italians, Haitians, Thais, and Iranians. Of the native Spanish-speaking students, those from the Dominican Republic make up the largest single group, Mr. Ferraro said, followed by Colombians, Venezuelans, and Ecuadorians.

All English classes are taught in English. The secretarial courses are taught in both English and Spanish.

Teaching English to the foreign born is the number one mission of the institute. Next comes the secretarial and skills courses, then the course to prepare for high school equivalency, and finally one on operation of keypunch machines.

Twenty percent of the students use the institute as a stepping stone to more training or an academic education.

Jorge Ferrandiz and Ruben Mayungo both hope to go to

college, for example, Mr. Ferrandiz, who arrived from Spain a year ago, wants to study computer science at either New York University or Hunter College, Mr. Mayungo, who emigrated from Colombia eight months ago, plans to attend a community college in February. Both students are enrolled in high-school-equivalency classes and are studying advanced English at the institute.

Elena Romero, who arrived from Colombia a month ago, aspires to be a lawyer. Miss Romero, who studied English in her native country, is taking English and Spanish stenography, typing and business English classes.

"Many of the people who come here are fully competent in office skills or are fully qualified nurses or beauticians in their own countries, but it does not do them any good because they didn't know English," Mr. Ferraro said.

To change that—to gain a working knowledge of English—the school has found that the average student must come to class four hours a day, five days a week, at a cost ranging from $1.66 to $2.12 per hour of instruction.

Many students support themselves in low-paying jobs in the garment district, which is one reason the institute has always been in the Times Square area, near the clothing center and well served by public transportation.

The biggest difference in operating the school now compared with the early days, Mr. Ferraro said, is the growing ease of student placement. "We get ten to twelve calls a week from employers looking for people who speak Spanish," he said. "I used to have to plead with people to give our graduates a chance."

The reason? "Today, the Spanish market cannot be ignored." Real-estate offices in New York and New Jersey need Spanish-speaking personnel, he said. Requests also come from banks, insurance companies, publishers, and unions.

Despite the demand for Spanish-speaking office workers, Mr. Schiffman said, there is still an anti-Hispanic bias. "People will say to me: Aren't you afraid to go to school? Aren't you afraid of being knifed?"

He and Mr. Ferraro say they have created an old-fashioned learning environment, the kind they knew at "old New Utrecht High." They say that in the Spanish-American Institute's twenty-five-year-history, no student has ever abused a teacher and there has never been a single case of vandalism.

"It is very nice, this school," said Yolanda Guevara, who emigrated from Ecuador seven months ago and is studying to become a bi-lingual secretary.

"Yes, they teach you nice," added Gina Ambrossi, who arrived from Ecuador three years ago and has been a student of the institute for a year. "Sure, I like it. That's why we're here. It is very good."

Copyright © 1980 by *The New York Times* Co. Reprinted with permission.